OTHER NITTY GRITTY COOKBOOKS

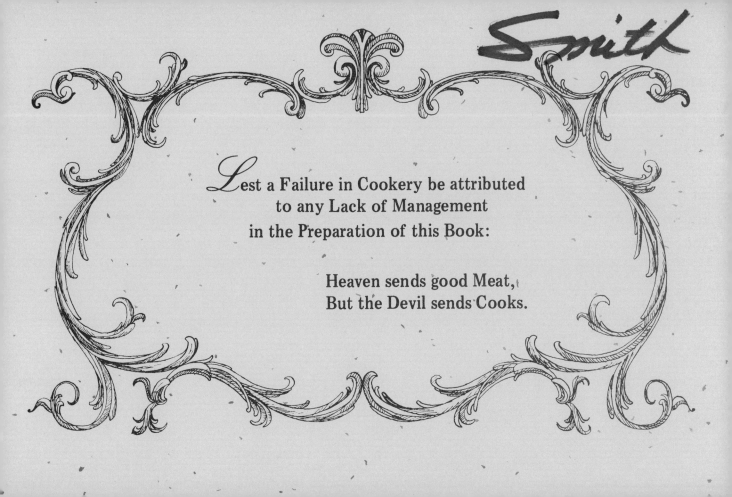

Smith

Lest a Failure in Cookery be attributed
to any Lack of Management
in the Preparation of this Book:

Heaven sends good Meat,
But the Devil sends Cooks.

The Compleat American Housewife

1776

By Julianne Belote

Illustrated By Craig Torlucci

© Copyright 1974
Nitty Gritty Productions
Concord, California

A Nitty Gritty Book*
Published by
Nitty Gritty Productions
P.O. Box 5457
Concord, California 94524

*Nitty Gritty Books — Trademark
Owned by Nitty Gritty Productions
Concord, California

Library of Congress Cataloging in Publication Data

Belote, Julianne.
    The compleat American housewife 1776.

    1. Cookery, American. 2. Home economics—United
States—History. 3. United States—Social life and
customs—Colonial period, ca. 1600-1775. I. Title.
TX715.B463   641.5'973   74-7257
ISBN O-911954-02-3

Table Of Contents

The Reader

On July 4, 1776, my marriage day, I entered the life of housewifery. As my thoughts were personal that day, I little understood, as the Journalist Mr. Paine has said, that "The birthday of a new world is at hand." Since that day I have striven to increase my knowledge of the duties and processes of American housewifery together with the ways of this American life from New England to the South.

Believing that no art ought to claim a Preference to that

which makes Life easy, my aim is to instruct Ladies in the Nicest ways of management, to cook the goodly variety of American stiles, and to join economy with elegance. My wish is that this collection of fine recipes of the most renowned cooks along with sentiments, instructions and observations of prominent citizens will advance the American Lady for her lasting pleasure and that of her family's.

Finally, I commend to you these views on cookery by the English author, Mrs. Glasse, and subscribe also to her hopes for your approval, dear Reader, in this instance, for an American wife.

If gentlemen will have French cooks they must pay for French tricks. I have heard of a French cook that used six pounds of butter to fry twelve eggs; when everybody knows that half a pound is full enough, or more than need be used; but then it would not be French. So much is the blind folly of this age, that they would rather be imposed on by a French booby, than give encouragement to a good American cook.

If I do not gain the esteem of those gentlemen let that be as it will. I shall say no more, only hope my Book will answer the ends I intend it for; to improve the servants, and save the ladies a great deal of trouble.

3

Women are creatures without which there is no comfortable living . . . it is true of them what is wont to be said of governments, that bad ones are better than none."

John Cotton

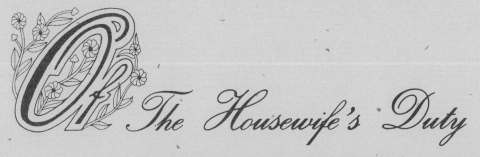

Of The Housewife's Duty

Since this treatise is calculated for the improvement of the rising generation of Females in America, these Hints are suggested for the more general and universal knowledge of those females, so that they may do those things which are essential to the perfecting them as good wives and useful members of society.

It is the province of the Housewife to be of chaste thoughts, stout courage, patient, untyred, watchfull, dilligent, witty, pleasant, constant in friendship, full of good Neighbour-Hood, wise in discourse but not frequent therein—sharp and quick of speech but not bitter or talkative, secret in her affaires, comfortable in her counsels, and generally skillful in the worthy knowledges which belong to her vocation.

These virtues remain in demand though fashion and fancy change. Observe this newspaper advertisment of a Pennsylvania farmer who needs a housekeeper: "Wanted at a Seat about half a day's journey from Philadelphia, on which are good improvements and domestics, A single Woman of unsullied Reputation, an affable, cheerful, and amiable Disposition; cleanly, industrious, perfectly qualified to direct and manage the female Concerns of country business, as raising small stock, dairying, marketing, combing, carding, spinning, knitting, sewing, pickling, preserving, etc., and occasionally to instruct two Young Ladies in those Branches of Oeconomy, who with their father, compose the family. Such a person will be treated with respect and esteem, and meet with every encouragement due to such a character."

If you are about to enter on the duties of a housekeeping life, the precepts of Mrs. Randolph of Virginia, famous Mistress of "Moldavia" and reputed to be the best cook in Richmond, will be of certain help.

"The prosperity and happiness of a family depend greatly on the order and regularity established in it. The husband, who can ask a friend to partake of his dinner in full confidence of finding his wife unruffled by the petty vexations attendent on the neglect of household duties—who can usher his guest into the dining-room assured of seeing that methodical nicety which is the essence of true elegance,—will feel pride and exultation in the possession of a companion, who gives to his home charms that gratify every wish of his soul, and render the haunts of dissipation hateful to him. Sons bred in such a family will be moral men, of steady habits; and daughters will each be a treasure to her husband; and being formed on the model of an exemplary mother, will use the same means for securing the happiness of her own family, which she has seen successfully practiced under the paternal roof."

The good manager should begin her day with an early breakfast, the whole family in attendance together for a social and comfortable meal. While the servants, if you have them, breakfast in the kitchen, you may employ yourself in washing the cups, glasses; arranging the cruets, the mustard, salt-sellers, pickle vases, and all the apparatus for the dinner table. The kitchen breakfast over, you should then go in to give your orders and have all the articles intended for dinner pass in review: have the butter, sugar, flour, meal, lard, given out in proper quantities, and whatever may be wanted for each dish, measured to the cook.

This procedure would ensure economy and relieve the mistress of the horrible drudgery of keeping house all day, when one hour devoted to it in the morning, would release her from trouble until the next day.

The grand arcanum of management can be stated in three simple rules: Let every thing be done at a proper time, keep every thing in its proper place, and put every thing to its proper use."

Mary Randolph of Virginia

The first requisite is to have a good cow. One that has high hips, short forelegs, and a large udder is to be preferred. The cream-colored and the mouse-colored cows generally give a large quantity and of rich quality. Her feeding should be faithfully attended to. She should have a good pasture not far distant, or if this is impracticable, care must be taken that she is not made to run—a piece of mischief frequently practiced. Giver her a teacupful of salt once a week.

10

Feed her once a day with the waste from the kitchen, adding to it about 1 pt. of Indian meal. Give her the skimmed milk not wanted in the family. If she does not readily drink it, teach her by keeping her a few days without an ample supply of water. Take care that nothing is given her which will injure the taste of the milk, such as turnips and parsnips. Carrots are a fine vegetable for cows. Have her milked by a person who understands the process, or she will not give it freely, and will soon become dry.

But the most abundant supply of the richest milk will avail little unless all the articles used in the care of it are kept in perfect order. They should not be used for other purposes. Keep a cloth for washing them only, and never wash them in the same water with other dishes. After washing, every article and the cloth with which they are washed must be scalded. Wash off thoroughly all the milk from the pans, pail, strainer, churn, dasher, skimmer, spoons, etc., before scalding them. If milk remains in them when scalded, the butter will be injured, as may be supposed from the fact that a cloth strainer, if scalded a few times with milk in it, becomes yellow and as stiff as if it were starched.

If a cloth strainer is used, it should be of thin, coarse linen. A basin having a fine wire strainer is used by many persons. Tin pails and pans are better than wood and earthen; because tin is more easily kept sweet than wood, and the glazing upon brown earthen pans is sometimes decomposed by sour milk. About 2 years ago four men, while making hay on a warm day, drank buttermilk which had been kept in a jar of potter's ware, and every one died immediately. Those who keep 1 or 2 cows only, will find a stoneware churn best. No other is so easily kept sweet.

Have the milk closet on the coolest side of the house, or in the dryest and coolest part of the cellar, and with a window in it covered with wire net or slats. Good butter cannot be made without a free circulation of fresh air. Every inch of such a closet must be kept perfectly clean.

Strain the milk as soon as it is brought in, and set immediately in its place. To remove milk after the cream has begun to rise prevents its rising freely. For the same reason the smallest quantity should not be taken from a pan set for raising cream; therefore all the milk wanted for the day's use must be set apart from the other pans. Skim the cream as soon as the milk has become loppord, which will, in hot weather, be in about thirty hours.

In very hot weather, especially in August, which is the least favorable month for making butter, 1 heaping teaspoonful of salt should be put into a pailful of milk, after the portion for the ordinary family use is taken out; and at all seasons, fine salt should be put into the cream from day to day, as it is gathered. The effect of this is excellent, in keeping it sweet and giving a rich flavor to the butter.

The finest butter is made where the number of cows renders it necessary to

12

churn every day. The custom of churning once a week is not to be tolerated. If you keep but 1 cow, churn twice a week; and in dog days, 3 times. Do it in the cool of the morning. If the weather is warm, set the churn into a tub of cold water; add ice if you have it, and put a piece also into the churn.

Air is necessary to make butter come; therefore, if the cream flies out of the opening around the dasher, do not put anything around to prevent it. When the butter has come, take it out into the wooden bowl with a ladle or skimmer.

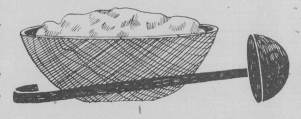

13

Work the butter with the ladle, until the buttermilk ceases to come out; then sprinkle it with clean sifted salt. Work it in well, and taste it to see if more should be added. Observation and experience must teach you how much to use. Mold the butter with the ladle into balls or lumps or any form you prefer; put it into a covered jar or tureen and set it in the icehouse or cellar.

The most celebrated housewife of our time is undoubtedly Martha Danridge Custis Washington. Though some say she is not socially scintillating, her kindness and dignity impress all. Even in the midst of her eminent position as our President's wife, she has been heard to describe herself as "an old-fashioned Virginia housekeeper, steady as a clock, busy as a bee, and cheerful as a cricket."

Her duties, as the wealthy mistress of Mount Vernon, are substantial. As part of her dower when she married the General in 1759 she brought one hundred fifty slaves. These, with those already on the estate who were not field hands, come under her particular care. Every small detail, from ordering the meals to directing the cooking, to determining where the pease shall be sown and in how many rows, is said to be under her careful supervision.

Though justly famous as a hostess, she is at heart a country aristocrat who can easily assume the privileges befitting her and her husband. At a recent party, she is reported to have concluded the evening by rising and announcing to her company, "The General always retires at nine, and I usually precede him."

We have an English proverb that says, 'He that would thrive must ask his wife' It was lucky for me that I have one as much dispos'd to industry and frugality as myself. She assisted me chearfully in my business, folding and stitching pamphlets, tending shop, purchasing old linen rags for the paper makers, etc.

We kept no idle servants, our table was plain and simple,— our furniture of the cheapest. One morning being call'd to breakfast, I found it in a china bowl with a spoon of silver! They had been bought for me without my knowledge by my wife. She thought her husband deserv'd a silver spoon and china bowl as well as any of his neighbours. This was the first appearance of plate and China in our house which afterwards in course of years, as our wealth increas'd, augmented gradually to several hundred pounds in value.

15

Dr. Franklin

It is not to be wondered that they continually run away and make poor laborers. Governor Mathew of the Leeward Islands has spoken of them as "poorly cladd, hard fedd, a worse state than a common soldier." And Elizabeth Sprigs writes of them "toiling day and night, and then tied up and whipped to that degree you would not beat an animal, scarce anything but Indian corn and salt to eat and that even begrudged."

While some are impudent and intolerabel saucy . . . take care to set him at liberty when his time expires and treat them with kindness.

17

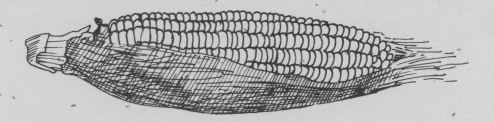

Always when you sweep a room, throw a little
wet sand all over it, and that will gather up all
the slew and dust, prevent it from rising,
clean the boards, and save the bedding, pictures,
and all other furniture from dust and dirt."

18

Abigail Adams, the wife of John Adams, is a housewife and hostess quite able to match wits with any man. In writing to her husband in 1776, she plainly expresses the new sense of confidence we women are achieving and how we too have interest in the Revolutionary movement.

" . . . in the new code of laws which I suppose it will be necessary for you to make, I desire you would remember the ladies, and be more generous to them than your ancestors. Do not put such unlimited power in the hands of husbands. Remember, all men would be tyrants if they could. If particular care and attention are not paid to the ladies, we are determined to foment a rebellion, and will not hold ourselves bound to obey the laws in which we have no voice or representation."

19

Of Colonial Life

My aim is to instruct the American lady beyond mere cookery, but also in the customs of our country from New England to the farthest South. Our differences are many because our origins are many, but our new nation requires of us a knowledge of these differences. Already sectional snobbery is in the air. Virginians say the ladies of Philadelphia are homely and hard favored; New Yorkers say Virginians live only to feast and riot; and they all say New Englanders lack grace and manners. Now that we have most bravely accomplished our Independence, we must turn to the task of bringing in Harmony the varieties of customs in these colonies.

There are those today who say travelling to our Southern colonies will take you into the midst of many dangerous temptations; gay company, frequent entertainment, little practical devotion, no remote pretention to heart religion, and daily examples in men of the highest quality of luxury, intemperence and impiety.

Such reports must be laid to envy. The mould of fashion is indisputably the Virginian or the Carolinian. He is celebrated justly not only for elegance in dress, speech, dining and sport, but for the way he excels in all the social arts. Unlike most of his compatriots, he has a fund of social small-talk. True, he does delight in fox hunting, cock fighting, horse-racing and dancing parties, but without him our century would be appreciably more gray, for with all his vanities, he has taste.

The gentlemen are partial to blue, the product of their staple indigo, while their wives and daughters dress in the latest French mode.

Until the Revolution, these planters called England "home" and many sent their sons there for schooling, but the practice is dying. A current joke about them is that they can read Homer and make a speech to explain the Constitution, but cannot do a sum in fractions. Such is an example of the jealousy about them.

There are many simple houses in the South, one story, unpainted and no panes of glass. But the successful planters live in some of the most beautiful houses ever built. The women of these large estates are more accomplished than you mistresses of small houses without slaves might imagine. She must supervise the running of the vast household, the cooking, clothmaking and the lavish entertaining. To demand the best of her help she must understand all the processes while employing also the social graces so valued here.

Food is abundant, of the finest quality, and elegantly served. Most keep well stocked wine cellars. Their hospitality is so extravagant it is fast becoming legendary. A traveller from London has written of Virginia, "All over the Colony,

23

an Universal Hospitality reigns; full Tables and open Doors, the kind Salute, the generous Detention, Speak Somewhat like the old Roast-beef Ages of our Fore-fathers . . . " Innkeepers complain they scarce can make a living so eager are the residents for guests and so lavish is their hospitality.

The kitchen is usually some fifty paces from the house, since gentry of the South believe—no matter the hazards of cold dishes—that cooking has no business under the same roof with eating.

Should you have the good fortune to be a guest at a fine plantation, or should you merely be curious, the daily life will proceed in this manner:

Upon waking, one finds that a servant has built the fire, brushed shoes and clothes, and now stands ready for further orders—for every visitor has an appointed black servant for his exclusive benefit. At eight o'clock one breakfasts with the family, on a table bare except for doilies under the plates, drinking first coffee and then tea, and eating cold ham of the real Virginia flavor with hot breads. Until one o'clock the guest rides or reads; then the gentlemen congregate to drink grog and the ladies to chat. Dinner is served at three. The mistress ladles soup at one end of the table, while her husband carves a saddle of mutton at the other. Black boys hand round dishes of ham, beef, turkey, duck, eggs and greens, sweet potatoes, and hominy. After a round of champagne the upper cloth is removed, and upon the damask beneath plum pudding, tarts, ice cream, and brandied peaches are served. When you have eaten this, off goes the second table cloth, and then upon the bare mahogany table is set the figs, raisins, and almonds, and before the host is set two or three bottles of wine—Madeira, Port, and a sweet wine for the ladies—he fills his glass and pushes them on. After a toast to the

ladies and the drinking of two glasses, the ladies themselves retire for an hour of music and chit-chat, while the gentlemen begin to circulate the bottle pretty briskly. Through the twilight the dinner guests drive home, while those remaining sit down to a rubber of whist, with a light supper and a night-cap to follow.

The Dutch women of New York are reputed to be less distinguished for social charm and grace than for thrift, initiative and commercial shrewdness. It is also said that every woman over forty smokes a pipe, but this may be exaggeration. They are much renowned for their clean households, surely a virtue to be admired. When Dr. Alexander Hamilton visited New York he wrote of their houses: "The Dutch here keep their houses very neat and clean, both without and within. Their chamber floors are generally laid with rough plank which, in time, by constant rubbing and scrubbing becomes as smooth as if it had been plained. Their chambers and rooms are large and handsom. They have their beds generally in alcoves so that you may go thro all the rooms of a great house and see never a bed. They affect pictures much, particularly scripture history, with which they adorn their rooms. They set out their cabinets and bouffetts much with china.

Their kitchens are likewise very clean, and there they hang earthen or delft plates and dishes all round the walls in manner of pictures, having a hole drilled thro the edge of the plate or dish and a loop of ribbon put into it to hang it by . . . They live here very frugally and plain, for the chief merit among them seems to be riches, which they spare no pains or trouble to acquire, but are a civil and

26

hospitable people in their way, but att best, rustick and unpolished. I imagined when I first came there that there were some very rich people in the place. They talked of 30, 40, 50 and 100 thousand pounds as of nothing, but I soon found that their riches consisted more in large tracts of land than in cash."

In the early days, the Dutch did not face starvation as did the New Englanders and their settlements have now reduced to a minimum the hardships of the New Land. Dr. Hamilton, who is used to the warmer Virginia climate did complain that "Their winter here is so excessive cold so as to freeze their cattle stiff in one night in the stables."

Still, houses are more colorful and life seems more gay than on farms in New England. Their comfort and snug living is due mostly to the wives. They do all necessary to support life. Besides the ordinary cooking she prepares delicious dainties and preserves. She draws perfumes from the flowers; she sees the hops are planted, dried and brewed; she culles herbs and concocks medicaments. In addition she supervises the carding and weaving and spinning.

Of special interest in Dutch houses is the little stoep, a high wide doorstep with benches built on each side. Another is the double door, with the upper and lower section separately hinged. Since pigs run at will through the villages and streets rooting in the garbage thrown there, the citizens have adopted this Dutch door. It keeps the pigs out and can be open at the top to let fresh air in.

For a gay social life, New York is fast becoming a rival to Philadelphia. The houses are tolerably well built and those along the Broad-Way have most of them a row of trees before them which form an agreeable shade and produce a pretty effect. It is known for the decency and cleanness of the place.

In Pennsylvania the barns are often such fine, high structures, they suggest the farm is the whole interest of the people, and indeed it seems to be. The Germans settled here have explained to their Quaker neighbors that they speak "deutsch" and have so mistakenly come to be called "Pennsylvania Dutch."

29

They love to eat and the wives are noted for their flavorful dishes with such odd sounding names as Schnitz and Knepp and Shoofly Pie.

Philadelphia is the center of the colony of Pennsylvania. Here the Quakers live, avoid war on principle and cultivate as far as possible the arts and advantages of peace. Plain though their stile has been, they advance steadily to more ornate and picturesque dress, causing one Quaker visitor to lament that they take so much liberty "in launching into finery."

The Quaker is a citizen and by preference he lives in town and generally engages in business. In the main, they are a thrifty and prosperous class, and they entertain with a lavish hand.

This plain Friend, with his plain but pretty wife with her Thees and Thous, had provided us a costly entertainment: ducks, hams, chickens, beef, pig, tarts, creams, custards, jellies, floats, trifles, floating islands, beer, porter, and wine."

Summer of 1776, John Adams

Some believe Philadelphia surpasses all other American cities in communal improvements. Many streets are paved in the middle for carriages with a footpath of hard brick on each side, and they are well illumined with lamps.

There are now over 4000 houses built in the city. Most are entirely of brick and generally three stories high and well sashed. Virginia ladies have been heard to complain of small rooms, but then, some are never satisfied.

I have heard the complaint "in general the manners of this place has more of bluntness than refinement and want those little attentions that constitute real politeness and are so agreeable to strangers." In truth, the rural life is hard and laborious and the New England wives work hard, mind their tongues and fear God. The spirit of Puritanism has still a clasp on the people and there is a general detestation of idleness. John Adams has spoken his scorn of the fashionable vogue for idle diversion: "Let others waste their bloom of life at the card or billiard table among rakes and fools."

In the country households of the North everything but a few items are obtained from the farm. One farmer has reported except for $10.00 spent for salt and iron, he "bought nothing to eat, drink, or wear, as my farm provided all."

New Englanders do not cook or entertain on the scale of the South, but they are exceedingly busy people with no slaves and few if any servants. All members of the family work as though they feared above all that, "The devil finds some mischief still for idle hands." Besides the work in the field and shops, there is the making of apple butter, cider, butter, cheese, soap and candles to be done. Even social affairs are most often combined with useful communal work such as house-raising, sheep-shearing, log-rolling and husking bees.

The heart of every house is the common room or the kitchen with the great fireplace. All through the long winter festoons of dried pumpkin chunks hang from the rafters on long strings and add a cheery note of color. Even common households possess an abundance of mugs and tankards, which suggest strong drink is their one indulgence.

Daily fare is pork, either salted or fresh, corn meal and from their bountiful waters, the cod and every other kind of fish. Many farm families have four meals a day, beginning with suppawn, sausage and pudding shortly after sunrise.

Boston may have the reputation of sobriety and decorum, nevertheless you

discover little difference between it and other places. Drinking and fighting occur not less than elsewhere; and as to truth and godliness, you must not expect more of them here than of other places. Every Farmer's Son, when he goes to the Market-Town, must have money in his purse; and when he meets with his companions, they go to the Tavern or Ale-house, and seldome away before Drunk, or well tipled. It is rare to find men that we call Drunkards, but there are abundance of Tiplers in New England. Its citizens know how to amuse themselves.

34

While Plays are not obtained here, card playing has won its way into almost complete favor. Ladies and Gentlemen dress and appear gay and people of Quality attend concerts and balls.

Despite Mr. Adams' scorn: "I never knew a dancer good for anything else." dancing is the principal and favorite amusement. The country people dance the jigs and reels; the Quality dance the minuet.

Among the most popular social occasions are funerals, to which public and private invitations are issued. One wag claims New Englanders attend at every opportunity because they are the only form of social gathering at which absolutely no one, under any circumstances is ever expected to be either amusing or amused.

Mr. John Adams, that New Englander of sterling merit, can be pardoned for his vanity when he wrote in 1774 from Philadelphia concerning his native Massachusets: "The morals of our people are much better; their manners are more polite and agreeable; they are purer English; our language is better, our taste is better, our persons are handsomer; our spirit is greater, our laws are wiser, our religion is superior, our education is better."

 Bread, All Sorts

Bread is that article of food of the first necessity, combining the sustaining powers of the animal and vegetable kingdom in one product. In these Colonies we have as many breads as there are fish in the sea. The good cook should know a variety and be skillful in the use of her brick oven.

When building your oven for baking, observe that you make it round, low roofed, and a little mouth; then it will take less fire, and keep in the heat better than a long oven and high roofed, and will bake the bread better.

First build a fire directly in it for the purpose of heating the walls. They must be got hot enough to hold enough heat long enough to complete your baking.

Your oven door must be left partly open to supply air to the fire, to allow smoke to escape, and to let the cook watch her fire.

For even heat, stir your fire and push it about to different spots on the oven floor. When the fire has burned to ashy coals, rake them out and test the heat with your hand. My own test has always been to thrust my hand and arm into the oven. If I can hold it there until I can count thirty and no longer, it is right. If the oven is too hot, you must allow it to cool: if you reckon it not hot enough, you must start again with another fire.

When the oven is right, put in your bread or things to be baked using your oven peel. Close the door and do not open it again until you judge the things to be done.

38

Many housewives having no brick oven will do all their baking on the hearth. You will learn with practice to turn out all sorts of delicious breads, pies and cakes by this method.

Sweep a clean spot on the hearth and place a piece of dough directly on the hot bricks. Cover it with an upsidedown pot of iron or earthenware, and then cover the pot with embers and pile hot coals around it. Experience will dictate the baking time needed.

39

The best wood for fuel in everybody's opinion is hickory. The white and black oaks are next in goodness.

The cook must take great care for the hazards surrounding the fireplace. The constant maintenance of a fire, the necessary raking apart of the embers and coals to provide a slow or gentle cooking temperature, the need to build up brisk flames to produce quick heat for other dishes, mean that even careful cooks risk daily injury. Sparks and bits of wood roll out onto the hearth and can quickly spark our skirts.

Take care that the lug-pole in your fireplace does not become too brittle and charred from too long use. If it breaks under the weight of a pot, human hide as well as the stew will be lost.

That woman is fortunate who has the new strong iron crane for her fireplace. It swings the kettle out from the fire very nicely and thus gives the cook the advantage of not getting burned so often.

From Mrs. Mary Holyoke's diary in 1778, you can see how even the experienced housewife can suffer many fires:

Jan. 29 Burnt kitchen and Back room chimney

Feb. 27 Burnt kitchen and Back room chimney

April 20 Burnt kitchen and Back room chimney

Oct. 2 I began a barrel of sugar

Oct. 12 Began a firkin of butter

Oct. 15 Began a Barrel of flour

Nov. 17 Burnt back room and kitchen chimney

Take 3 quarters of a peck of fine flower & strow salt in as much as will season it, then heat as much milke as will season it luke warme, hould it high when you poure it on to make it light, & mingle with your milke 4 or 5 spoonfulls of good yeast, worke your paste well, & then let it ly a rising by the fire, your oven will be heated in an houre & halfe then shut it up a quarter of an houre, in which space make up your loaves & then set them in the oven, an houre & halfe will bake them.

TO MAKE A BUTTERED LOAFE

Take 4 quarts of milke put runnit to it & whey it & hang the curd up in a cloth to dreyne for an houre or 2, then take 10 eggs & leave out 3 of the whites then take a little ginger, a pinte of ale yeast, as much fine flowre as will make it up to a loafe. When it is well baked cut it up, & butter it with sweete butter & sugar your butter must be melted & beat up with the sugar before your put it into your loafe.

42

The matter of keeping on hand a supply of good yeast requires good management. The preferred kind is barm, the froth that forms on the top of fermenting ale or beer.

Don't wool gather—gather wood.

Take a lump of dough, about two pounds of your last making, which has been raised by barm, keep it by you in a wooden vessel, and cover it well with flour. This is your leaven; then the night before you intend to bake, put the said leaven to a peck of flour, and work them well together with warm water. Let it lye in a dry wooden vessel, well covered with a linen cloth and a blanket, and keep it in a warm place. This dough kept warm will rise again next morning, and will be sufficient to mix with two or three bushels of flour, being worked up with warm water and a little salt.

This delicious hot bread would doubtless not exist at all if it were not for the kitchen slaves of the South. To achieve just the right texture and lightness the dough must be beaten hard. If the biscuits are intended for everyday eating, three hundred whacks are sufficient, but if company is coming for dinner, no less than five hundred will do! One opinion expressed to me is that a colored boy about twelve years old is the best beater, and the time should be more nearly an hour than a half hour.

44

Place on a smooth flat surface of a tree stump and beat with an iron pestle or side of a hatchet until the dough raises little blisters of air and is smooth and satiny.

BEATEN BISCUIT

Take one Quart of Flour, Lard the Size of a Hen's Egg, one Teaspoonful of salt. Make into a moderately stiff Dough with sweet Milk. Beat for half an Hour. Make out with the Hand or cut with the Biscuit Cutter. Stick with a Fork and bake in a hot Oven, yet not sufficiently hot to blister the biscuit.

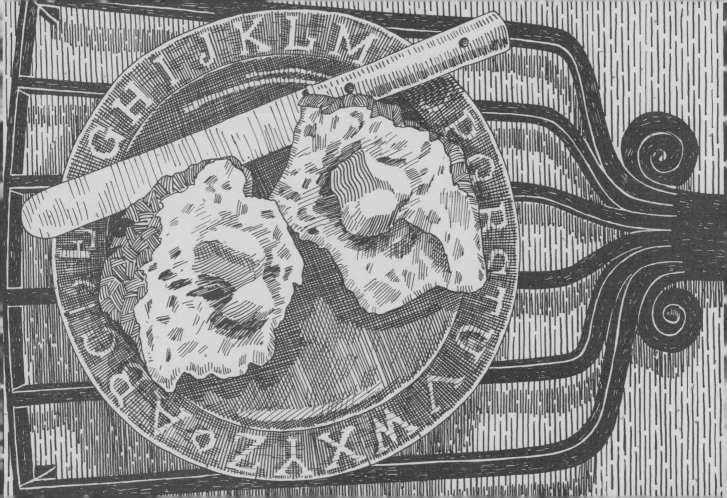

SWEET POTATO BUNS

Boil and mash a potato, rub into it as much flour as will make it like bread—add spice and sugar to your taste, with a spoonful of yeast; when it has risen well, work in a piece of butter, bake it in small rolls, to be eaten hot with butter, either for breakfast or tea.

TO MAKE A NICE BISCUIT

46

Rub a large spoonful of butter into a quart of risen dough, knead it well, and make it into biscuit, either thick or thin: bake them quickly.

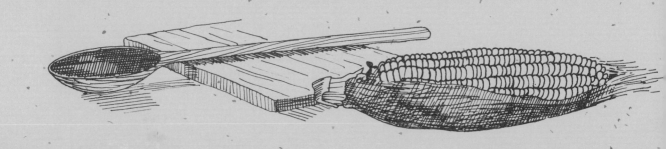

Ryaninjun is the name of the steamed brown bread that always accompanies beans to New England tables. For the amusement of the cook, I have found this recipe in rhyme.

Three cups of corn meal
One of rye flour;
Three cups of sweet milk,
One cup of sour;
A cup of molasses
To render it sweet,
Two teaspoons of soda
Will make it complete.

Take a quart of milk, beat in six or eight eggs, leaving half the whites out; mix it well till your batter is of a fine thickness. You must observe to mix your flour first with a little milk, then add the rest by degrees; put in two spoonfuls of beaten ginger, a glass of brandy, a little salt; stir all together, make your stew-pan very clean, put in a piece of butter as big as a walnut, then pour in a ladleful of batter, which will make a pancake, moving the pan round that the batter be all over the pan, shake the pan, and when you think that side is enough, toss it; if you cannot, turn it cleverly; and when both sides are done, lay it in a dish before the fire, and so do the rest. You must take care they are dry; when you send them to table strew a little sugar over them.

48

This is a Thing very easy to a bold hand, but which a timerous Person will never be able to do well; for such a one, she is to know that the first Thing to be done is to get rid of her Fear, and then a little Practice will make it quite familiar.

The best Way to learn it is this:

Let a Kitchen Table Cloth be spread upon the Ground at a small Distance from the Fire, and when the first Pancake is ready for turning let the Cook try to toss it over the Cloth; if it falls in right it is very well, and if not there is no Harm done, it will be catched clean, and may do for the Servants Table.

When there is not the Danger of throwing them into the Fire the Cook will have less Fear, and as we have said before, the less Fear the more Likelihood of Success.

The Way is to hold the Pan very steady, and toss the Pancake with a sudden Jerk.

Practice is all; for as the Children play at Bilbecket till they can catch the Ball every Time for many Minutes together, in the same Manner the Cook will be able to toss a hundred Pancakes without missing once, when she is accustomed to the Method of it.

Christopher Ludwick has a bakeshop famous in Philadelphia. The aristocracy eat his gingerbread, almond cakes and marzipan and order his cakes for their parties. Back when the war came, this plump man, who looks not unlike the caricatures of King George III, served the cause of a free America baking for the troops. He substituted corn meal for the more costly wheat flour and molasses for sugar. "Give me the corn, sir," he said to General Washington, "and your troops will be fed."

51

Mrs. Randolph of Richmond makes a corn bread mixing flour and corn meal:

Take six spoonsful of flour and three of corn meal, with a little salt—sift them, and make a thin batter with four eggs, and a sufficient quantity of rich milk; bake it in little tin moulds in a quick oven.

She also has a receipt for corn meal bread without flour:

52

Rub a piece of butter the size of an egg, into a pint of corn meal—make it a batter with two eggs, and some new milk—add a spoonful of yeast, set it by the fire an hour to rise, butter little pans, and bakt it.

Cooks in the North like to sweeten their corn bread with a little sugar.

Our citizens both high and low, mean and genteel love Johnny Cakes. The recipes have bounced around until no one can agree on the authentic ingredients. Our first colonists learned to make them from the Indians and called them Shawnee cakes. They are also called Journey Cakes since travelers often take packages of them on long trips.

Scald 1 pint of milk and put to 3 pints of indian meal, and half pint of flour—bake before the fire. Or scald with milk two thirds of the indian meal, or wet two thirds with boiling water, add salt, molasses and shortening, work up with cold water pretty stiff, and bake as above.

2 lbs. flour; 1/2 lb. butter; 3 eggs; 3/4 lb. sugar; 1 nutmeg; 1/2 cup milk; 1 tsp. saleratus*; add flour lastly and it will not usually require the full amount. Make one day, bake the next.

*Salaratus is a new ingredient lately come into the markets in Philadelphia and New York. It will perform miracles in your baking.

MOLASSES

Molasses is the poor man's substitute for sugar as well as the stuff from which rum is made. Little wonder we were in such an uproar when England put a revenue duty on molasses from the West Indies. Parliment had to back down, of course, reducing the impost.

As you know all during the war sugar and molasses were both so scarce, one had to sweeten according to one's own idea of economy. All patriots gladly ate simple dishes, and even now we still rejoice that dining again has become something to talk about.

55

I know not why we should blush to confess that molasses was an essential ingredient in American independence.

John Adams

 *Soups*

A good hot soup or broth bubbling in the pot is ever welcome. It soothes the stomach and encourages it to receive more nourishment. It is satisfying for people who are hungry, as well as for those who are tired, worried, cross, in debt, in love or in pain. Even a useless piece of meat can be used if you boil it, extract all its juices and serve a stimulating broth. People threatened with overweight should eat only plain broth.

First take great care the pots or sauce-pans and covers be very clean and free from all grease and sand, and that they be well tinned, for fear of giving the broths and soups a brassy taste. If you have time to stew as softly as you can, it will both have a finer flavour, and the meat will be tenderer. But then observe, when you make soups or broths for present use, if it is to be done softly, do not put much more water than you intend to have soup or broth; and if you have the convenience of an earthen pan or pipkin, set it on wood embers till it boils, then skim it, and put in your seasoning; cover it close, and set it on embers, so that it may do very softly for some time, and both the meat and broths will be delicious. You must observe in all broths and soups that one thing does not taste more than another; but that the taste be equal, and that it has a fine agreeable relish, according to what you design it for; and you must be sure, that all the greens and herbs you put in be cleaned, washed, and picked.

Boil a knuckle of veal to a jelly strain it off—and season it as you please, put to it the body & tails of 3 lobsters a pint of white wine—make balls of the claws finely beaten and the yolks of 2 eggs, nutmeg, pepper and salt—boil them—and then fry them in butter and put them in ye soop.

TO MAKE PEAS-PORRIDGE

Take a quart of green peas, put them to a quart of water, a bundle of dried mint, and a little salt. Let them boil till the peas are quite tender; then put in some beaten pepper, a piece of butter as big as a walnut, rolled in flour, stir it all together, and let it boil a few minutes; then add two quarts of milk, let it boil a quarter of an hour, take out the mint, and serve it up.

59

PHILADELPHIA PEPPER POT

Philadelphia Pepper Pot is the soup of our American Revolution. It was improvised for General Washington's troops wintered at Valley Forge. With food scarce and the weather cruel, the story goes the General asked the cook to prepare something hot and filling for his cold, hungry troops. Having only some tripe, some peppercorns and scraps, the cook invented this soup that reportedly met with great approval.

Now that our scarcities are over, many other ingredients are usually added, but tripe is always used, cut in small cubes and simmered with other vegetables.

In Philadelphia now, Negro women go through the streets selling pepper pot, their approach announced with the call, "Peppery pot, smokin' hot!"

Place tripe, a veal shank, three quarts of water and salt in a large, heavy pot. Bring to boyle, then simmer and scum it. Boyle it softly two hours. Remove the meat from the broth and cut it from the bones and into chunks. Add onions, carrots, celery, green pepper, and parsley with meat and Irish potatoes to the broth. Tie up your cloves and peppercorns in a square of cloth and add it to the broth. Cover close and bring to boyle, then simmer as necessary for all to be tender. Serve up to a good family of 12 if they eat not excessively.

60

The only way in which they are eatable.

Put the fowls in a coop and feed them moderately for a fortnight; kill one and cleanse it, cut off the legs and wings, and separate the breast from the ribs, which, together with the whole back, must be thrown away, being too gross and strong for use. Take the skin and fat from the parts cut off which are also gross. Wash the pieces nicely, and put them on the fire with about a pound of bacon, a large onion chopped small, some pepper and salt, a few blades of mace, a handful of parsley, cut up very fine, and two quarts of water, if it be a common fowl or duck—a turkey will require more water. Boil it gently for three hours, tie up a small bunch of thyme, and let it boil in it half an hour, then take it out. Thicken your soup with a large spoonful of butter rubbed into two of flour, the yolks of two eggs, and half a pint of milk. Be careful not to let it curdle in the soup.

61

Take a leane piece of beefe, a piece of veale or muton & a hen & boyle them in a pot & scum them, put in some large mace & halfe a cabbage if a little one, some sweet hearbs, as lettice & spinnage &c. boyle them well till all the goodness be out, then put in the bottom of a house-hould lofe, toward the end roste a leane piece of beef & cut it often for gravie, draine your broth clear from the bottom & boyle some pigeons in salt & water & save a piece of cabbage to put in the middle of your dish. Let it stand on coles, after the pigeons gravie & broth is in.

AN ONION SOUP CALL'D THE KING'S SOUP

(Though the name of this soup is these days out of favor, it was most popular before the Revolution and is still a good soup. I have heard it is often on the menu at Mount Vernon.)

Slice 2 large onions, add a quart of milk, some mace blade, a large spoonful of butter, some salt and put it all in a pot. Bring it to a boil then cook slowly until the onions are very tender. Pick out the mace blades and discard. Beat an egg yolk in a small bowl and add a little of the hot soup, beating it. Pour the mixture back into the soup pot and cook a few minutes longer.

63

Of Flesh and Fish

It is natural that man should seek to feed on flesh; he has too small a stomach to be supported alone by fruit. In this country, plain boiling and roasting are the usual cooking methods. While we depend on some form of flesh daily for strength, it grows scarce in war time and habit makes it a worrisome expense. It is agreed that fish is much less nourishing than red meat because being lighter in weight for the same bulk, it has less substance. Yet these sea animals offer us an agreeable variety for our table.

The general rules are, to have a brisk hot fire, to hang rather than to spit, to baste with salt and water, and one quarter of an hour to every pound of beef, tho' tender beef will require less, while old tough beef will require more roasting; pricking with a fork will determine you whether done or not; rare done is the healthiest of this age.

A BEEF-STEAK PIE

66

Beat rump Steak with a rolling Pin, then season them with Pepper and Salt according to your Palate. Make a good Crust, lay in your Steaks filling your Dish therewith, and then pour as much Water in as will half fill the Dish. You may put in the hard-boiled yolks of six or eight Eggs, if you chuse it. Put on the Top Crust and bake it well.

I wish the Bald Eagle had not been chosen as the Representation of our Country; he is a Bird of bad moral Character, like those among men who live by sharpening and robbing, he is generally poor and often very lousy . . . The turkey is . . . a much more respectable bird, and withal a true original native of America.

Benjamin Franklin

67

Bone them, and make a force-meat thus: take the flesh of a fowl, cut it small, then take a pound of veal, beat it in a mortar, with half a pound of beef sewet, as much crumbs of bread, some mushrooms, truffles and morels cut small, a few sweet herbs and parsley, with some nutmeg, pepper, and salt, a little mace beaten, some lemon-peel cut fine; mix all these together, with the yolks of two eggs, then fill your turky, and roast it. This will do for a large turky, and so in proportion for a fowl. Let your sauce be good gravy, with mushroom, truffles and morels in it: then garnish with lemon, and for variety sake you may lard your fowl or turky.

Grate a wheat loaf, one quarter of a pound butter, one quarter of a pound salt pork, finely chopped, 2 eggs, a little sweet marjoram, summer savory, parsley and sage, pepper and salt (if the pork be not sufficient,) fill the bird and sew up.

The same will answer for all Wild Fowl.

Water Fowls require onions.

The same ingredients stuff a leg of Veal, fresh Pork or a loin of Veal.

69

Take some parsley shred fine, a piece of butter as big as a walnut, a little pepper and salt; tie the neckend tight; tie a string round the legs and rump, and fasten the other end to the top of the chimney-piece. Baste them with butter, and when they are enough lay them in the dish, and they will swim with gravy. You may put them on a little spit, and then tie both ends close.

A PRETTY WAY OF STEWING CHICKENS

70

Take two fine chickens, half boil them, then take them up in a pewter, or silver dish, if you have one; cut up your fowls, and separate all the joint-bones one from another, and then take out the breast-bones. If there is not liquor enough from the fowls add a few spoonfuls of water they were boiled in, put in a blade of mace, and a little salt; cover it close with another dish, set it over a stove or chafing-dish of coals, let it stew till the chickens are enough, and then send them hot to the table in the same dish they were stewed in.

You may do rabbits, partridges, or moorgame this way.

In Virginia the most popular standing dish is a boiled joint, the famous Virginia-cured ham. Contemporary tastes all through the colonies now agree that any large cut of meat—a leg, loin, breast, neck rump or haunch—should be put into cold salted water and placed over a large clear fire for steady, even cooking.

Boiling is the Dressing Things by Means of Water, as Roasting does it by the naked Fire; this is the whole Difference, but in general Boiling is the easiest Way, as it requires less Nicety and Attendance. To keep the Water really boiling all the Time, to have the Meat clean, and to know how long is required for doing the Joint, or other Thing boiled, comprehends almost the whole Art and Mystery.

71

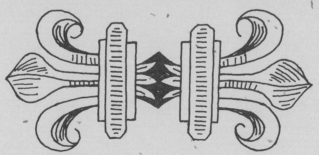

TO BOIL A NEAT'S* TONGUE

A dried tongue should be soaked over night, when you dress it, put it into cold water and let it have room; it will take a least four hours. A green tongue out of the pickle need not be soaked, but will require near the same time. An hour before you dish it up, take it out and blanch it, then put it into the pot again till you want it, this will make it eat the tenderer.

*Calf

72

TO BOIL A LEG OF PORK

A leg of pork must lie in salt sixx or seven days after which put it into a pot to be boiled, without using any means to freshen it. It requires much water to swim in over the fire, and also to be fully boiled; so that care should be taken that the fire do not slacken while it is dressing. Serve it with melted butter, mustard, buttered turnips, carrots or greens.

Parboil your cocks-combs, then open them with a point of a knife at the great end: take the white of a fowl, as much bacon and beef-marrow, cut these small, and beat them fine in a marble mortar; season them with salt, pepper, and grated nutmeg, and mix it with an egg; fill the cocks-combs, and stew them in a little strong gravy softly for half an hour; then slice in some fresh mushrooms and a few pickled ones; then beat up the yolk of an egg in a little gravy, stirring it. Season with salt. When they are enough, dish them up in little dishes or plates.

73

Beat it well with a rolling pin in its own blood. Cut it into little bits and fry them. Then put the hare into a stew pan with a quart of strong gravy, pepper and salt according to the palate, and let it stew till tender. Thicken it with butter and flour. Serve it up in its gravy with sippets in the dish and lemon sliced for garnish.

74

Having cased the hare, turn the blood out of the body into the jug. Then cut the hare to pieces, but do not wash it. Then cut three quarters of a pound of fat bacon into three slices.

Pour upon the blood about a pint of strong, old, pale beer: put into the jug a middling sized onion stuck with three or four cloves, and a bunch of sweet herbs. And having seasoned the hare with pepper, salt and nutmeg, and lemon peel grated, put in the meat, a layer of hare, and a layer of bacon. Then stop the jug close, so that the steam be kept in entirely.

Put the jug into a kettle of water over the fire, and let it stew three hours, then strain off the liquor, and having thickened it with burnt butter, serve it up hot, garnished with lemon sliced.

75

A meat stew that can be preserved several days by keeping it slowly simmering at the back of the hearth has always found great favor with colonial cooks. Brunswick Stew is one of those delectable things that benefit from long, slow cooking. Its flavor improves if it is left to stand overnight and reheated.

Everyplace named Brunswick from Canada to the Carolinas tries to claim this stew as its own, but Brunswick County, Virginia has the best claim. It is a hearty meal and one of the principle attractions at political rallies, cockfights, tobacco-curings and all outdoor gatherings. With squirrels plentiful, this dish is of good economy.

77

Cut up two Squirrels and put in a large Pan with three quarts of water, one large sliced onion, one half pound of lean Ham cut in small pieces and simmer gently for two hours. Add three pints of tomatoes, one pint of lima beans, four large Irish potatoes diced, one pint corn, salt and pepper according to the palate and a small pod of red pepper. Cover and stew softly, till ready.

*Bad dinners
go hand in hand
with total depravity,
while a man properly fed
is already half-saved.*

TO STEW A COD

Cut ye cod in thin slices and lay them one by one in the bottom of the stewpan—put a pint of white wine, half a pound of butter, some oysters, and their liquor 2 or 3 blades of mace, a few crumbs of bread (or pounded bisquit) pepper and salt—let it stew till enough done Garnish with sliced lemon.

TO CURE TAINTED FISH

Tainted fish may be much restored to its proper flavor by mixing a quantity of vinegar and salt in the water in which the fish is to be boiled.

79

FOR DRESSING CODFISH

Put the fish first into cold water, and wash it, then hang it over the fire and soak it six hours in scalding water, then shift it into clean warm water, and let it scald for one hour. It will be much better than to boil.

Being becalm'd off Block Island, our people set about catching cod, and hauled up a great many. Hitherto I had stuck to my resolution of not eating animal food and on this occasion I consider'd the taking of every fish as a kind of unprovoked murder ... But I had formerly been a great lover of fish, and when this came hot out of the frying-pan, it smelt admirably well. I balanc'd some time between principle and inclination, till I recollected that, when the fish were opened, I saw small fish taken out of their stomach's; then thought I, 'If you eat one another, I don't see why we mayn't eat you.' So I din'd upon cod very heartily ... So convenient a thing it is to be a reasonable creature, since it enables one to find or make a reason for every thing one has a mind to do.

Benjamin Franklin

The claim is made, and I shall repeat it here, of the special virtues of soft clams, or "Man of Noses" as those in Carolina call them. An English visitor to the colony says:

They are valued for increasing vigour in men, and making barren Women fruitful, but I think they have no need of that Fish; for the Women in Carolina are fruitful enough without their Helps.

TO DRESS A PIKE CARPE TUB OR LARGE TROUT

Take your fish & scale it & slyt it alive & wash it with white wine, & take the blood & as much white wine as will cover it, putting a fish plate in the bottom of your kettle, & some large mace with a bundle of sweet hearbs, as time parsley & sweet margerum, let it have one boyle then take it of and let stew leasurely, then bone 5 anchovis & put into the liquor, then take 3 quarters of a pound of good fresh butter, & let them stew together a little while, then take up your fish & shake up your butter anchovis & broth alltogether & poure it on your fish & dish it up with sippets.

82

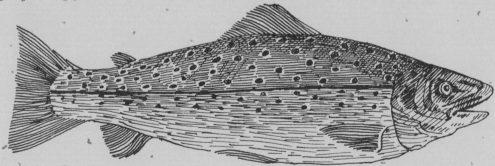

TO RECOVER VENISON WHEN IT STINKS

Take as much cold water in a tub as will cover it a handful over, and put in good store of salt, and let it lie three or four hours. Then take your venison out, and let it lie in as much hot water and salt, and let it lie as long as before. Then have your crust in readiness, and take it out and dry it very well, and season it with pepper and salt pretty high, and put it in your pastry. Do not use the bones of your venison for gravy, but get fresh beef or other bones.

TO MAKE BEST BACON

To each ham put one ounce salt-petre, one pint bay salt, one pint molasses, shake together six or eight weeks, or when a large quantity is together, baste them with the liquor every day. When taken out to dry, smoke three weeks with cobs or malt fumes.

83

Of Garden Stuff

Nowhere in the world do people have such a variety of good garden things to grow and eat as in these colonies. Still our daily fare can be monotonous. How beneficial it would be if more of our countrymen thought as freely as does Mr. Thomas Jefferson about fruits and vegetables. Since he was a young boy Mr. Jefferson has kept garden records of the plantings at his home and has been curious about every vegetable, exotic or ordinary.

Most people spoil garden things by over-boiling them. All things that are green should have a little crispness, for if they are over-boiled, they neither have any sweetness or beauty.

TO BOIL FRENCH BEANS

86

Take your beans and string them, cut in two, then across, when you have done them all, sprinkle them over with salt, stir them together, as soon as your water boils put them in and make them boil up quick, they will be soon done and they will look of a better green then when growing in the garden; if they are very young, only break off the ends, then break in two and dress them in the same manner.

Take young peas, shell them, put them in a cullender to drain, then lay a cloth four or five times double on a table, then spread them on, dry them very well and have your bottles ready, fill them, cover them with mutton suet fat when it is a little soft; fill the necks almost to the top, cork them, tie a bladder and a leather over them and set them in a dry cool place.

NEW ENGLAND BAKED BEANS

87

Put a quart of white beans to soak in soft water at night: the next morning wash them out,—put them in a pot with more water than will cover them, let them simmer on fire till quite tender, wash them out again, and put them in an earthen pot; scald and gash 1-1/2 lbs. of pork; place it on top of the beans so as to have the rind even with the beans; fill the pot with water in which 2 tablespoons of molasses are mixed. Bake five or six hours. If baked in brick oven it is best to have them stand over night.

Indian corn is considered the most important food staple in America. It is our chief mainstay—our everlasting diet all over the colonies.

Some early opinions were that the barbarous Indians knew no better and by necessity thought it good food. Foolish colonists thought it a more convenient food for swine than for man. Sensible leaders, however, faced with grim and grizzled starvation, quickly learned to cultivate and harvest their own plots of corn and so kept themselves alive.

88

Lest any among us forget, during the starving times, it was corn that kept our first colonists alive. Many in Europe disdain our American grain, but the good Dr. Franklin set them right. He spiritedly defended the virtues of corn in a letter to a London newspaper in 1766 during the dispute over the stamp act.

"... a writer in your paper comforts himself, and the India Company, with the fancy that the Americans, should they resolve to drink no more tea, can by no means keep that Resolution, their Indian corn not affording 'an agreeable, or easy digestible breakfast.' Pray let me, an American, inform the gentleman, who seems ignorant of the matter, that Indian corn, take it for all in all, is one of the most agreeable and wholesome grains in the world ... and that johny or hoecake, hot from the fire, is better than a Yorkshire muffin ... Mr. Vindex's very civil letter will, I dare say be printed in all our provincial news-papers ... and together with the other kind, polite and humane epistles of your correspondents ... contribute not a little to strengthen us in every resolution of advantage, to our country at least, if not yours."

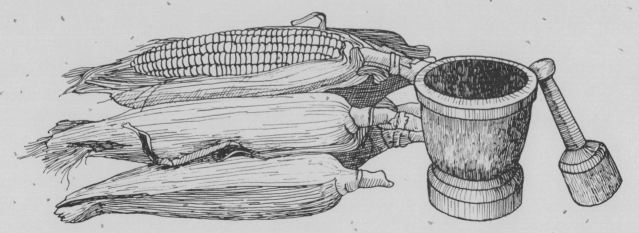

From corn comes the most notable standing dish in all the colonies and saved us from starvation—Indian pudding, that which some call Hasty pudding or loblolly or Suppawn. In truth, for the cook, there is nothing hasty about this pudding of corn meal mixed with water or milk. Many farm families eat such a pudding twice every day of the year. For the main course it is served with milk, and for dessert, sweetened with molasses or maple syrup.

"Come at Pudding time," means in most colonies, come in time for dinner. Puddings are brought to the table before the meat and vegetables at Sunday dinners in the home of John Adams and other New Englanders. The place of pudding on the menu even enters into political life. The Federalists eat their puddings first, but the Democrats begin their dinners with meat.

90

Fath'r and I went down to camp
Along with Captain Goodin,
And there we saw the men and boys
As thick as hasty puddin'.

The young men of Harvard College are devotees of Hasty Pudding. Since the Revolution, undergraduates have started a new club called "Hasty Pudding." Activities center around dinner at a certain Cambridge inn on "hasty pudding night."

BOILED INDIAN PUDDING

Mix one quart of corn meal, with three quarts of milk; take care it be not lumpy—add three eggs and a gill of molasses; it must be put on at sun rise, to eat at three o'clock; the great art in this pudding is tying the bag properly, as the meal swells very much.

BAKED INDIAN MEAL PUDDING

Boil one quart of milk, mix in it two gills and a half of corn meal very smoothly, seven eggs well beaten, a gill of molasses, and a good piece of butter; bake it two hours.

Of all the puddings we colonial wives have boiled and baked, the first was pumpkin. We have sliced them, dried them and hung them from the kitchen beams. We have cut them into a dice, filled pots with them and stewed them all day. So many pumpkins have we stewed, boiled and baked, one settler composed this bit of verse:

We have pumpkins at morning, and pumpkins at noon,
If it were not for pumpkins we should be undone.

PUMPKIN PUDDING

Stew a fine sweet pumpkin till soft and dry; rub it through a sieve, mix with the pulp six eggs quite light, a quarter of a pound of butter, half a pint of new milk, some pounded ginger and nutmeg, a wine glass of brandy, and sugar to your taste. Should it be too liquid, stew it a little drier, put a paste round the edges, and in the bottom of a shallow dish or plate—pour in the mixture, cut some thin bits of paste, twist them, and lay them across the top, and bake it nicely.

Boil one pound of sweet potatoes very tender, rub them while hot through a colander; add six eggs well beaten, three quarters of a pound of powdered sugar, three quarters of butter, and some grated nutmeg and lemon peel, with a glass of brandy; put a paste in the dish, and when the pudding is done, sprinkle the top with sugar, and cover it with bits of citron. Irish potato pudding is made in the same manner, but is not so good.

93

The Indians use them much, boyling them with Sugar for Sauce to eat with their Meat, and it is a delicate Sauce, but expensive because of the sweetening required. They are brought to market every Wednesday and Saturday at Philadelphia late in autumn.

Wash a quart of cranberries and remove the stems and wilted berries. Put them with 2 cups of sugar and 2 cups of water and boil without stirring until the skins burst. Cool and serve up with your meat.

94

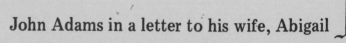

Pray how does your aspargus perform?

John Adams in a letter to his wife, Abigail

Apples are highly useful in families ... There is not a single family but might set a tree in some otherwise useless spot, which might serve the two fold use of shade and fruit; on which 12 or 14 kinds of fruit trees might easily be engrafted and essentially preserve the orchard from the intrusions of boys, &c, which is too common in America.

If the boy who thus planted a tree, and guarded and protected it in a useless corner, and carefully engrafted different fruits, was to be indulged free access into orchards, whilst the neglectful boy was prohibited—how many millions of fruit trees would spring into growth ... The net saving would in time extinguish the public debt, and enrich our cookery.

Take a dozen good pippins, cut them in half and core. Place them in a tight mazarine dish with the skins on, the cut side down; put to them a little water, scrape on them some brown lump sugar. Put in a hot oven till the skins are burnt black, and your apples are tender. Serve them on plates with a good cow cream.

To extinguish a fire in the chimney, besides any water at hand, thro on it salt, or a handful of flowers of sulfur, as soon as you can obtain it; keep all the doors and windows tightly shut, and hold before the fireplace a blanket, or some woolen articles to exclude the air.

Pare six pears, and either quarter them or do them whole: they make a pretty dish with one whole, the rest cut in quarters, and the cores taken out. Lay them in a deep earthen pot, with a few cloves, a piece of lemon peel, a gill of red wine, and a quarter of a pound of fine sugar.

If the pears are very large, they will take half a pound of sugar, and a half a pint of red wine; cover them close with brown paper, and bake them till they are enough.

98

Serve them up hot or cold, just as you like them, and they will be very good with water in the place of wine.

MRS. HORRY'S PRESERVED PEACHES

Take the peaches full grown and ripe but not soft, weigh them to every pound of peaches take 1/2 sugar. (Slice) the peaches very thin and put them in a jar sprinkling sugar between every layor of peaches, let them lay 12 hours in which time the juice will be drawn. Then put them in some preserving jar and boil them till transparent then put them in bottles or small jars putting in 2 or 3 glasses of Brandy to each while warm.

N.B. When you do a good many peaches 1/2 sugar to a pound is sufficient, but if only 2 or 3 (pounds) it will require 3/4 to each pound.

99

Very good.

The fruits that are most fit for preservation in syrup are, apricots, peaches, nectarines, apples, greengages, plums of all kinds and pears. Boil them up three days successively, skimming each time, and they will then be finished and in a state fit to be put into pots for use.

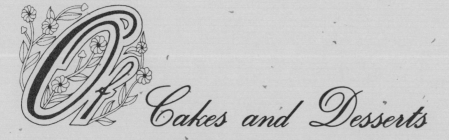

Of Cakes and Desserts

The dessert certainly repays, in its general effect, the expenditure upon it of much pains; and it may be said, that if there be any poetry at all in meals, or the process of feeding, there is poetry in the dessert, the materials for which should be selected with taste. The garnishing needs special attention. Many consider a dessert incomplete without candied and preserved confections in elegant forms.

Take forty eggs and divide the whites from the yolks, and beat them to a froth.

Then work four pounds of butter to a cream, and put the whites of the eggs to it, a tablespoonful at a time, until it is well worked.

Then put four pounds of sugar, finely powdered, to it in the same manner.

102

Then put in the yolks of eggs and five pounds of flour and five pounds of fruit.

Two hours will bake it.

Add to it one-half an ounce of mace, one nutmeg, one-half pint of wine and some French brandy.

This was made by Martha Custis for her grandmama.

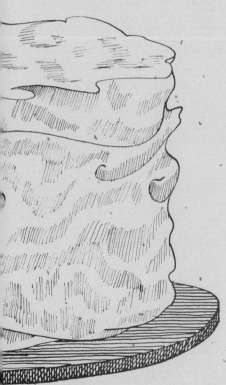

Take the whites of twenty-four eggs, and a pound of double-refined sugar beat and sifted fine; mix both together in a deep earthen pan, and with a whisk whisk it well for two or three hours, till it looks white and thick; then with a thin broad board, or bunch of feathers, spread it all over the top and sides of the cake; set it at a proper distance before a good clear fire, and keep turning it continually for fear of its changing colour; but a cool oven is best, and an hour will harden it. You may perfume the icing with what perfume you please.

103

Take a pound of butter, beat it in an earthen pan with your hand one way, till it is like a fine thick cream; then have ready twelve eggs, put half the whites; beat them well, and beat them up with the butter, a pound of flour beat in it, a pound of sugar, and a few carraways. Beat it all well together for an hour with your hand, or a great wooden spoon, butter a pan and put it in, and then bake it an hour in a quick oven.

For a change, you may put in a pound of currants, clean washed and picked.

104

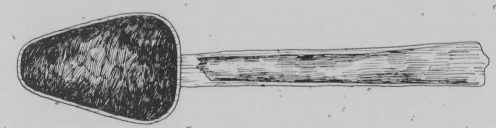

Martha Washington is an excellent hostess and is said to possess a notebook of handwritten recipes given to her by Mrs. Custis, the mother of her first husband. Her dinners are famous and she is particularly noted for the art of preparing fruit and custard pyes.

Our fruit-filled dessert pies are very much an American development. Most families eat them several times a week—especially enjoyed at breakfast. While pye to the English has always meant a meat pye baked with a pastry crust top, these sweet pyes are our American invention.

Puff paste is the nicest crust. If you have not fresh fruit available, only lay in your preserved fruit, and put a very thin crust at top, and let them be baked as little as possible.

is the Desrt that graces all the Feast,
For an ill end disparages the rest . . .

Rub half a pound of butter fine with a Gallon of Flour, and a little salt. Make it up into a light Paste with cold Water, just stiff enough to work it well up; then roll it out, and stick small pieces of butter all over the paste, strewing a little flour upon it from a drudging Box or your hand; then roll it up together, and with a rolling Pin roll it out again flat and untill it is about half an Inch thick, and so do, nine or ten times, and untill you have rolled into your Paste about a pound and a half of butter. This is the crust that is most usually found in good Pies of all kinds.

106

... if rightly made, is a thing of beauty and a joy—while it lasts. Two inches deep is better than the thin plasters one sometimes sees. With the pastry tender, and a generous filling of smooth spiced sweetness—a little trembly as to consistency, and delicate brown on top—eat a liberal cut before the life has gone out of it.

Pare a Pumpkin, and take the seedy part of it out; then cut it in slices; Pare and core a quarter of an hundred of apples, and cut them in slices. Make some good paste with an Egg, and lay some all around the Brim of the Dish; lay half of a pound of good, clean Sugar over the bottom of your Dish, over that a Layer of apples; then a Layer of Pumpkin, and again so untill the Pie is full, observing to put Sugar between every two Layers, and all the remaining Sugar on top. Bake it half an hour, and before you send it to the Table, cut it open and put in some good fresh butter.

RULES TO BE OBSERVED IN MAKING PUDDINGS

Let your pudding Cloth, or Bag, in which you tie up your boiled Puddings, be very clean, free from all Grease and Soap, well rinsed out. Before you put your Pudding in, dip your pudding Cloth in hot Water and flour it well. And observe as a general Rule, ever to Strain your Eggs that you beat for Puddings. If you boil your Puddings in Bowls or Shapes, butter the inside before you put in your Batter and be-sure that you fill them brimfull.

TO MAKE AN ORANGE PUDDING

Take the yolks of sixteen eggs, beat them well, with half a pound of melted butter, grate in the rind of two Seville oranges, beat in half a pound of fine sugar, two spoonfuls of orange-flower water, two of rose-water, a gill of sack, half a pint of cream, two Naples biscuits, or the crumb of a halfpenny roll soaked in the cream, and mix all well together. Make a thin puff-paste, and lay all over the dish and round the rim, pour in the pudding and bake it. It will take about as long baking as a custard.

Dessert jellies such as Flummery are much in favor and very elegant when served in special glasses. Isinglass is the purest form of gelatine, but most cooks find that calves' feet produce a better consistency and flavor if proper care be taken in the preparation.

Take a large calfs foot, cut out the great bones, and boil them in two parts of water; then strain it off and put to the clear jelly half a pint of thick cream, two ounces of sweet almonds, and an ounce of bitter almonds, well beaten together. Let it just boil, and then strain if off, and when it is cold as milk from the cow, put it into cups or glasses.

109

Colonists from England call this dessert the Trifle, but in this country the common folk call it Tipsy Squire and Tipsy Parson. This is Mrs. Randolph's way to do it:

Put slices of Savoy cake or Naples biscuit at the bottom of a deep dish; wet it with white wine, and fill the dish nearly to the top with rich boiled custard; season half a pint of cream with white wine and sugar; whip it to a froth—as it rises, take it lightly off, and lay it on the custard; pile it up high and tastily—decorate it with preserves of any kind, cut so thin as not to bear the froth down by its weight.

110

BLANC MANGE

To an ounce of Isinglass pour a Pint of boiling Water to stand Overnight. Next morning add three Pints of sweet Milk, a Pound and a quarter of loaf Sugar, and a Tablespoonful or two of Rose-water. Put it in a Brass Kettle, boil fifteen or twenty Minutes very fast; wet your Moulds and pour it in.

TO CANDY ROSE LEAVES TO LOOK FRESH

Take of the fayrest rose leavs red or damask and sprinkle them with rose water & lay them one by one, on white paper on a hot sunshiney day then beat some double refind sugar very small & sift it thinly on the roses, through fine laune sive & they will candy as they ly in the hot sun then turne the leaves & strow some rose water on the other side, & sift some sugar in like manner on them, turne them often sometimes strowing on water, & sometimes sifting on sugar till they be enough, then lay them in boxes betwixt clean papers & soe keep them all the year.

111

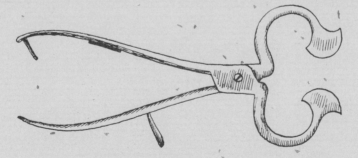

Of Health Drinking

Most colonists take to water as a last resort. As soon as our first apple crops are harvested, they are pressed into the cider that remains the chief beverage at every meal. It is said that John Adams drinks a tankard of hard cider every day before breakfast.

It is true throughout the colonies that everyone drinks liquor, from ministers to babes. The rare total abstainer is looked upon with suspicion by his neighbors. At a town meeting in Massachusetts it was declared with vehemence that liquor is absolutely essential to farm workers morale.

Lest some of you be disturbed by the amount of spirits our citizens drink, consider all the reasons: the water is oft times tainted and sometimes frozen over in winter; the weather can be cruel and work endless, and spirits seem to help people carry their burdens with more cheer. Then too, we mostly come from traditions where we were accustomed to refuse water in favor of beer and ale. Remember too, we have been using spirits much longer than the coffee and tea so much the fancy in these times. And for all of it—our vices are still less than those of Europe..

There's but one Reason I can Think,
Why people ever cease to drink,
Sobriety the Cause is not,
Nor Fear of being deam'd a Sot,
But if Liquor can't be got.

The frothy wine drink, Syllabub, traditionally served at Christmas is a favorite all through the colonies. The best recipe is this one from the American author Amelia Simmons.

TO MAKE A FINE SYLLABUB FROM THE COW

Sweeten a quart of cyder with double refined sugar, grate nutmeg into it, then milk your cow into your liquor, when you have thus added what quantity of milk you think proper, pour half a pint or more, in proportion to the quantity of syllabub you make, of the sweetest cream you can get, all over it.

Some cooks who need not reckon with economy, use white wine instead of cyder, and beat with their cream for half an hour.

115 𝕽𝕽

A very pretty drink for weddings and feasts is sack-posset. It is a combination of ale and sack, thickened with cream and eggs. Sugar, mace, and nutmeg are used for seasoning. After all these ingredients are mixed together, the mixture is boiled over the fire for several hours.

The New York Gazette carried this recipe in rhyme in 1744.

116

From famed Barbadoes on the Western Main
Fetch sugar half a pound; fetch sack from Spain
A pint; and from the Eastern Indian Coast
Nutmeg, the glory of our Northern toast,
O'er flaming coals together let them heat
Till the all-conquering sack dissolves the sweet.
O'er such another fire set eggs, twice ten,
New born from crowing cock and speckled hen.
Stir them with steady hand, and conscience pricking
To see the untimely fate of twenty chicken.
From shining shelf take down your brazen skillet,
A quart of milk from gentle cow will fill it
When boiled and cooked, put milk and sack to egg,
Unite them firmly like the triple League.
Then covered close, together let them dwell
Till Miss-twice sings, "You must not kiss and tell."
Each lad and lass snatch up their murdering spoon,
And fall on fiercely like a starved dragoon.

The days are short, the weather's cold,
By tavern fires tales are told.
Some ask for dram when first come in.
Others with flip and bounce begin.

In a 1 quart pitcher 2/3 full of strong beer, add enough sugar or molasses to give the beer a sweet taste. Then put enough rum in the pitcher to fill it, about 1/2 pint. Then heat the mixture by stirring it with a red-hot poker.

We do not wish to gossip, but pass on only as interesting information—Gen'l H. tells us that Gen'l Washington notwithstanding his perfect regularity and love of decorum can bear to drink more wine than most people. He loves to make a procrastinated dinner—makes it a rule to drink a glass of wine with everyone at table and yet always drinks 3-4 or more glasses of wine after dinner, according to his company.

Pare and slice a number of turnips, put them into a cider press, and press out all the juice. To every gallon of the juice, add three pounds of lump sugar; have a vessel ready large enough to hold the juice, and put half a pint of brandy to every gallon. Pour in the juice and lay something over the bung for a week, to see if it works; if it does, do not bung it down till it has done working; then stop it close for three months, and draw it off into another vessel. When it is fine, bottle it off.

This is an excellent wine for gouty habits, and is much recommended in such cases in lieu of any other wine.

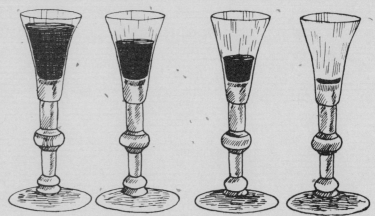

119

No nation is drunken where wine is cheap,
and none sober, where the dearness of wine substitutes
ardent spirits as the common beverage . . .

Thomas Jefferson

There is in Philadelphia a famed fishing and social club for gentlemen called the Fish House Club. A young Carolinian visiting the city wrote me about a rousing evening he had at the club testing their renowned punch:

"They have a Drink there called Fish House Punch. It is most Exslent if taken in Moderation, but it is so Smooth that One who does not know its Powers is likely to take too much. I Suppose I must have Drunk too much of it, but it did not Seem so at the Time. Next Morning was a Different Story."

121

FISH HOUSE PUNCH

Dissolve a pound of sugar in the smallest possible amount of cold water, then stir in a quart of lemon juice. Then add 2 quarts of rum, 1 quart of cognac, and 1/2 cup of peach brandy. Allow this to mellow for several hours, giving it a stir now and then.

To 12 pounds of parsnips, cut in slices, add 4 gallons of water; boil them till they become quite soft. Squeeze the liquor well out of them, run it through a sieve, and add to every gallon 3 pounds of loaf sugar. Boil the whole three quarters of an hour, and when it is nearly cold, add a little yeast. Let it stand for ten days in a tub, stirring it every day from the bottom, then put it into a cask for twelve months: as it works over, fill it up every day.

122

Oh we can make liquor to sweeten our lips
Of pumpkins, of parsnips, of walnut-tree chips.

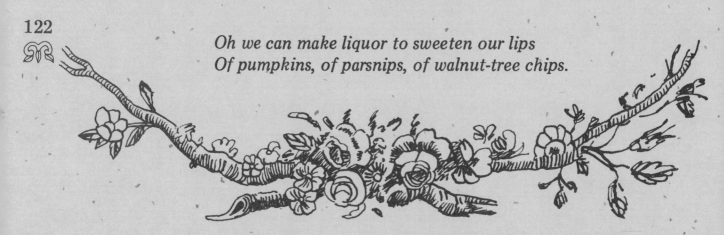

TAVERNS

A word about taverns—those centers of much of Colonial life and affairs. In peacetime, they are houses of sociability and entertainment, including theatrical productions, bear and turkey shoots. During the Revolution, they played their roll as court-rooms, prisons, barracks, hospitals and secret meeting places.

123

If you spent the evening in a tavern, you found it full of people drinking drams of flip, carousing, and swearing. The old taprooms were certainly cheerful and inviting gathering-places; where mine host sat behind his cagelike counter surrounded by cans and bottles and glasses, jars of whole spices and whole loaves of sugar; where an inspiring row of barrels of New England rum, hard cider, and beer ranged in rivalry at an end of the room.

John Adams

A barmaid, one Betsy Flanagan, is credited with the invention of the American cocktail. Her bar at the inn Halls Corners in Elmsford, New York was decorated with the brightly colored tail feathers of cocks. It was in 1776 that Betsy had the fanciful notion of adding a cock tail feather, as a sort of stirrer to each drink.

124

*At noon went to William Jones
to drink punch,
met several of my friends
and got decently drunk.*

From the diary of a Philadelphia gentleman

Patriots gave up tea even before the War because of the hated tax. In place of our beloved tea, our teapots steamed with peculiar brews, it must be admitted, made from such things as golden rod, sage or blackberry leaves. A recipe of the day advised, "The first leaves of the common currant bush, gathered at once and dried on tin, can hardly be distinguished from green tea." A foreign visitor to my tea table observed it was a "detestable drink," but one which Americans "had the heroism to find good."

Since few hostesses can boast a set of china cups, when a lady goes to a tea party she should carry her own cup, saucer and spoon. Then one nicely pours the hot tea from the cup and sips daintily from the saucer.

125

Every housewife, of course, longs for white sugar to serve. If you can order only one cone of it a year, do reserve it for festive occasions. A sugar cutter is very helpful in cutting the rocklike chunks into dainty pieces.

While Ladies groups all over the colonies signed pledges to abjure tea, this anti-tea poem appeared in several American newspapers shortly before the war:

Farewell the Tea-board with your gaudy attire,
Ye cups and ye saucers that I did admire;
To my cream pot and tongs I now bid adieu;
That pleasure's all fled that I once found in you.
Farewell pretty chest that so lately did shine,
With hyson and congo and best double fine;
Many a sweet moment by you I have sat,
Hearing girls and old maids to tattle and chat; . . .
No more shall my teapot so generous be
In filling the cups with this pernicious tea,
For I'll fill it with water and drink out the same,
Before I'll lose LIBERTY that dearest name,
Because I am taught (and believe it is fact)
That our ruin is aimed at in the late act,
Of imposing a duty on all foreign Teas,
Which detestable stuff we can quit when we please. . .

DURING THE WAR

There is a great scarcity of sugar and coffee, articles which the female part of the State is very loath to give up, especially whilst they consider the scarcity occassioned by the merchants having secreted a large quantity. . . . It was rumored that an eminent stingy wealthy merchant (who is a bachelor) had a hogshead of coffee in his store which he refused to sell the committee under six shillings per pound. A number of females, some say a hundred . . . marched down to the warehouse and demanded the keys which he refused to deliver. Upon which one of them seized him by his neck and tossed him into the cart . . . he delivered the keys when they tipped up the cart and discharged him; then opened the warehouse, hoisted out the coffee themselves, put into the trunks, and drove off. A large concourse of men stood amazed, silent spectators of the whole transaction.

128

From Abigail Adams' description at the time

Coffee accelerates digestion corrects crudities, removes colic and flatulencies. It mitigates headaches, cherishes the animal spirits, takes away listlessness and languor, and is serviceable in all obstructions arising from languid circulation. It is a wonderful restorative to emaciated constitutions, and highly refreshing to the studious and sedentary.

The habitual use of coffee would greatly promote sobriety being in itself a cordial stimulant; it is a most powerful antidote to the temptation of spirituous liquors.

It will be found a welcome beverage to the robust labourer, who would despise a lighter drink.

ARRACK: A spirit distilled in the East from rum.

CAUDLE: A kind of warm drink for sick persons; a mixture of wine or ale with eggs, bread or gruel, sugar, and spices.

COBBLER: Made of wine, sugar, orange or lemon

CORDIAL: An aromatized and sweetened spirit, used as a beverage.

CREAM: A syrupy liqueur.

CRAM, OR DRACHM: A small drink or draft

ELIXIR: A compound tincture or medicine; the refined spirit.

FLIP: Spiced, sweetened drink of ale beer, or the like to which beaten egg is sometimes added.

HIPPOCRAS: A highly spiced wine.

LIQUEUR: A spirituous liquor flavored with aromatic substances.

NECTAR: Sweet liquid secreted by the nectaries of a plant; the drink of the Gods.

POSSET: A beverage of hot milk, curdled as by ale, wine, &c, and spiced.

PUNCH: Usually composed of wine or distilled liquor, water, milk or tea, with sugar, lemon and often spice or mint.

RATAFIA: Any liqueur flavored with fruit kernals, especially of bitter almond.

SPIRITUOUS: Containing, or of the nature of spirit (alcohol); as spirituous liquor.

TAMARIND: A tropical tree, the fruit or pod of which has an acid pulp and is used for preserves and a laxative drink.

TANKARD: A tall, one handled drinking vessel; especially of pewter or silver with a lid.

TODDY: A mixture of spirit and hot water, sweetened, as a rum toddy.

TREACLE: A sovereign remedy; a cure. English molasses, which drains from sugar refining molds.

WINE: The fermented, or, loosely, the unfermented, juice of any fruit or plant used as a beverage.

131

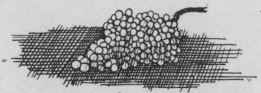

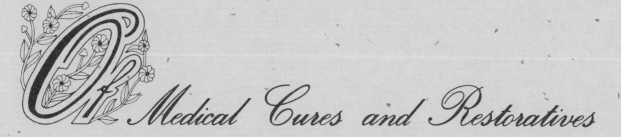

Of Medical Cures and Restoratives

While the author does not wish to presume to meddle in the physical way, she feels surely the Doctor would not think it improper to give a few directions for the Cook or Nurse. After all, everyone knows a good broth is a certain restorative at the beginning of a decline, or when any weakness is the complaint.

Every home should have its medicine chest and the sensible wife will stay alert to new cures. Madame Smith has written me from Virginia that the juice of Jerusalem Oak has cured all the negro children on the plantation of a distemper and that several negroes had drunk as much as half a pint of it at a time.

TO MAKE BEEF OR MUTTON BROTH FOR VERY
WEAK PEOPLE WHO TAKE BUT LITTLE NOURISHMENT

Take a pound of beef, or mutton, or both together: to a pound put two quarts of water, first skim the meat and take off the fat; then cut it into little pieces, and boil it till it comes to a quarter of a pint. Season it with a very little corn of salt, skim off all the fat, and give a spoonful of this broth at a time. There is greater nourishment from this than anything else.

134

TO MAKE BREAD-SOUP FOR THE SICK

Take a quart of water, set it on the fire in a clean sauce-pan, and as much dry crust of bread cut to pieces as the top of a penny-loaf, the drier the better, a bit of butter as big as a walnut; let it boil, then beat it with a spoon, and keep boiling it till the bread and water is well mixed; then season it with a very little salt, and it is a pretty thing for a weak stomach.

Take an ounce of beef-suet, half a pint of milk, and half a pint of water, mix them together with a table-spoonful of wheat-flour, put it over the fire ten minutes, and keep it stirring all the time, and take a coffe-cup full two or three times a-day.

A CERTAIN CURE FOR THE BITE OF A MAD DOG

Let the patient be blooded at the arm nine or ten ounces. Take of the herb called in Latin lichen cinereus terrestris, ash-coloured, ground liverwort cleaned, dried, and powdered, two drachms. Mix these well together, and divide the powder into four doses, one of which must be taken every morning lasting, for four mornings successively in half a pint of cow's milk warm. After these four doses are taken the patient must go into the cold bath, or a cold spring or river every morning lasting for a month. After this he must go in three times a week for a fortnight longer.

Mr. Hawes Green Oil

Take of the tops of red sage in flower, Rosemary in flower, Baum, Green Chamemile, Wild Valerian root & Eight Ounces of the best Olive Oil; Infuse three pints for ten days or a fortnight & two or three spoonfulls of this Oil, taken inwardly is very good in any inwards Bruises or Spitting blood & Cases in the dread Palsey If attended with a Cough.

136

For Consumption—take Valerian root dried & made into tea.

For a Cough—Take Three pints of Water abt half an Ounce of Liquorish one Ounce of Raisons in the Sun stoned two fige Sliced in a little Barley boiled till it comes to quart then strain it off.

Go not for every grief to the Physician,
nor for every quarrel to the lawyer,
nor for every thirst to the pot.

For a Fever—Take Salt or Wormwood three Drams put it into a large Bason and pour upon it six Spoonfulls of Juice of Lemons, and stir them together with a spoon till the fermentation is Over. then add to it half a Pint of white wine & water Equall parts & sweeten it with fine Sugar and take a wine glassfull every four hours. Purge & bleed.

A Gargle for a Sore Throat—Take Honey one Spoonfull Desolve it in half a pint of sage Tea. Then add two Spoonfulls of Vinegar, Brandy or Rum: three Spoonfulls of Salvolatile, Two or three spoonfulls—Gargle your throat three or four times a day warm—But don't neglect to Purge with a mana* & Glauber Salt & Bleed in time if Violent.

*a gentle laxative to buy from the pharmacy.

# Of Marketing Directions

To say everything that is useful to prepare a good table would swell this treatise too much, but I may be pardoned for making these few suggestions to the Lady who goes to Market.

In Marketing, that the best articles are the cheapest, may be laid down as a rule; and it is desirable, unless an experienced servant be kept, that the mistress should herself purchase all provisions needed for the house.

I have been distressed to see how embarrassed and tongue-tied some citizens become when they must deal with Merchants. Afterall, any trader can give himself the title of Merchant and you have no need to stand in Awe of him, unless you be indebted to him.

When he asks you how you will pay for your goods, there are four ways: <u>Pay</u> is Grain, Pork, Beef &c. at the prices sett by the General Court that Year; <u>Mony</u> is pieces of Eight, Ryals, or Boston or Bay Shillings (as they call them) or Good hard money, as sometimes silver coin is termed; also Wampon, viz. Indian beads which serves for change. <u>Pay as Mony</u> is provisions, as aforesaid one third cheaper than as the Assembly or General Court Sett it; and <u>Trust</u> is as you and the merchant agree for time.

Now when you ask for a comodity, sometimes before the merchant answers that he has it, he says, is Your pay redy? When you answer, then the price is sett.

Do not stand speachless till you are askt what you want, but serve yourself well and speak boldly.

How to chuse butchers meat

Lamb

In a fore-quarter of lamb mind the neck-vein; if it be an azure blue it is new and good, but if greenish or yellowish, it is near tainting, if not tainted already. In the hinder-quarter, smell under the kidney, and try the knuckle; if you meet with a faint scent, and the knuckle be limber, it is stale killed. For a lamb's head, mind the eyes; if they be sunk or wrinkled, it is stale; if plump and lively, it is new and sweet.

141

Veal

Veal is soon lost—great care therefore is necessary in purchasing Veal bro't to market in panniers, or in carriages is to be preferred to that bro't in bags, and glouncing on a sweaty horse . . . If the bloody vein in the shoulder looks blue, or a bright red, it is new killed; but if blackish, greenish, or yellowish, it is flabby and stale. If wrapped in wet cloths, smell whether it be mushy or not.

Beef

If it be right beef, it will have an open grain; if young, a tender and oily smoothness; if rough and spungy, it is old, or inclining to be so, except neck, brisket, and such parts as are very fibrous. A carnation pleasant colour betokens good spending meat, the suet a curious white: yellowish is not so good.

Pork

If it be young, the lean will break in pinching between your fingers, and if you nip the skin with your nails, it will make a dent.

Venison

Try the haunches or shoulders under the bones that come out, with your finger or knife, and as the scent is sweet or rank, it is new or stale. Look on the hoofs, and if the clefts are very wide and rough, it is old; if close and smooth it is young.

To know whether a Capon is a True one, young or Old, New or Stale

If he be young his spurs are short, and his legs smooth; if a true capon a fat vein on the side of his breast, the comb pale, and a thick belly and rump; if new, he will have a close hard vent; if stale, a loose open vent.

To Chuse the Best Fish

Every species generally of salt water fish are best fresh from the water, though the Hannah Hill, Black Fish, Lobster, Oyster, Flounder, Bass, Cod, Haddock and Eel, with many others may be transported by land many miles, find a good market, and retain a good relish; but as generally live ones are bought first, deceits are used to give them a freshness of appearance, such as peppering the gills, wetting the fins and tails, and even painting the gills with animal blood. Experience and attention will dictate the choice of the best. Fresh gills, full bright eyes, moist fins and tails denotes their being fresh caught; if they are soft, it is certain they are stale, but if deceits are used, your smell must approve or denounce them, and be your safest guide .

Salmon

The noblest and richest fish taken in fresh water—the largest are the best. They are unlike almost every other fish, are ameliorated by being 3 or 4 days out of water, if kept from heat and the moon, which has more injurious effect than the sun . . .

To Chuse Butter, Cheese and Eggs

When you buy butter, trust not to that which will be given you to taste, but try in the middle, and if your smell and taste be good, you cannot be deceived.

Cheese is to be chosen by its moist and smooth coat. If any soft or perished place appear on the outside, try how deep it goes, for the greater part may be hid within.

Eggs hold the great end to your tongue; if it feels warm, be sure it is new; if cold, it is bad, and so in proportion to the heat and cold, so is the goodness of the egg. This is a sure way not to be deceived. As to the keeping of them, pitch them all with the small end downwards in fine woodashes, turning them once a week end ways, and they will keep some months.

Roots and Vegetables

We proceed to Roots and Vegetables—and the best cook cannot alter the first quality, they must be good, or the cook will be disappointed.

Potatoes

take rank for universal use, profit and easy acquirement. The smooth skin, known by the name of How's Potatoe, is the most mealy and richest flavor'd. All potatoes should be dug before the rainy seasons in the fall, well dryed in the sun, kept from the frost and dampness during the winter, in the spring removed from the cellar to a dry loft, and spread thin, and frequently stirred and dryed, or they will grow and be thereby injured for cookery.

Onions

The Medeira white is best in market, esteemed softer flavored, and not so fiery, but the high red, round hard onions are the best; if you consult cheapness, the largest are the best, if you consult taste and softness, the very smallest are the most delicate and used at the first tables.

Beets

The red is the richest and best approved; the white has a sickish sweetness, which is disliked by many.

Garlicks

Tho' used by the French, are better adapted to the uses of medicine than cookery.

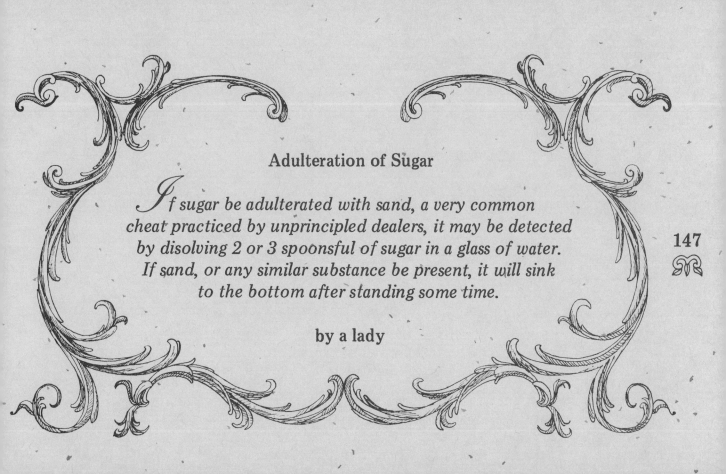

Adulteration of Sugar

If sugar be adulterated with sand, a very common cheat practiced by unprincipled dealers, it may be detected by disolving 2 or 3 spoonsful of sugar in a glass of water. If sand, or any similar substance be present, it will sink to the bottom after standing some time.

by a lady

147

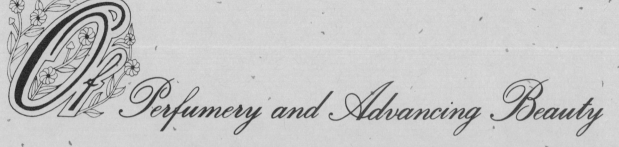

Of Perfumery and Advancing Beauty

If it be true that the face is the index of the mind, the recipe for a beautiful face must be something that reaches the soul. What can be done for a human face that has a sluggish, sullen, arrogrant, angry mind looking out of every feature. An habitually ill-natured, discontented mind ploughs the face with inevitable marks of its own vices. However bright its complexion, no such face can ever become really beautiful.

This receipt is said to be the very one used for the Virgin Queen's perfume: 8 grains Musk, put into 8 spoonfuls Rosewater with 3 spoonfuls of Damask Water and a quarter of an ounce of sugar. Boil 5 hours and strain.

Rose Water

Altogether you will want 3 pounds of rose petals. Put 2 or 3 cups of petals in a pot, then add a slight amount of water to keep them from burning and cover the pot tight. Then cook softly over the fire for half and hour. Then remove the petals and replace them with a like amount of fresh petals. Only add more water if it be necessary. Repeat this process until all the petals are used up. Strain the liquid into pots and keep them 3 days befor you use them.

Rose Leaf Pillow

To well-dried rose petals and sweet basil, add dried mint and pounded cloves. Mix well and stuff a small pillow with the mixture to induce sleep and fragrant dreams.

Magic Perfume

A perfume made of Hempseeds, Fleawort seeds, Violett root too and parsley; or, a mixture of Violet root and wild Parsley makes, (so it is said) men see into the future.

151

To Make Lip Salve

Take half a pound of hog's lard, put it into a pan, with one ounce and a half of virgin wax; let it stand on a slow fire till it is melted; then take a small tin-pot, and fill it with water, and put therein some alkanet-root; let it boil till it is of a fine red colour; then strain some of it, and mix it with essence of lemon; pour it into small boxes and smooth the top with your finger.

152 A Stick to Take Hair Out by the Roots

Take two ounces and a half of rosin, and one ounce of bees-wax; melt them together, and make them into sticks for use.

French Rouge—Five Shillings per pot

Take some carmine, and mix it with hair-powder to make it as pale as you please, according to your fancy.

Cold Cream

Melt one ounce oil of almonds, half-ounce spermaceti; one drachm white wax, and then add two ounces of rose water and stir it constantly until cold.

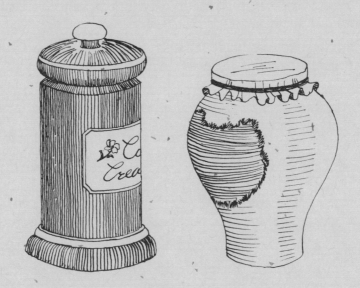

Hair Brightener

Beat 4 eggs whites to a froth. Rub them throroughly into the scalp and leave them to dry. Wash them out and rinse with equal parts rum and rose water. This is one of the best cleansers and brighteners of the hair that was ever used.

This very old receipe was brought from Europe and is still used by many genteel ladies for their hands:

154

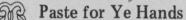

Paste for Ye Hands

Take a pound of sun raysens, stone and take a pound of bitter Almonds, blanch ym and beat ym in a stone morter with a glass of sack take ye peel of one lemond, boyle it tender; take a qyart of milk, and a pint of Ale and make therwith a Possett; take all ye Curd and putt it to ye Almonds; yn putt in ye Rayson: Beat all these till they come to a fine paste, and put in a pott, and keep it for ye use.

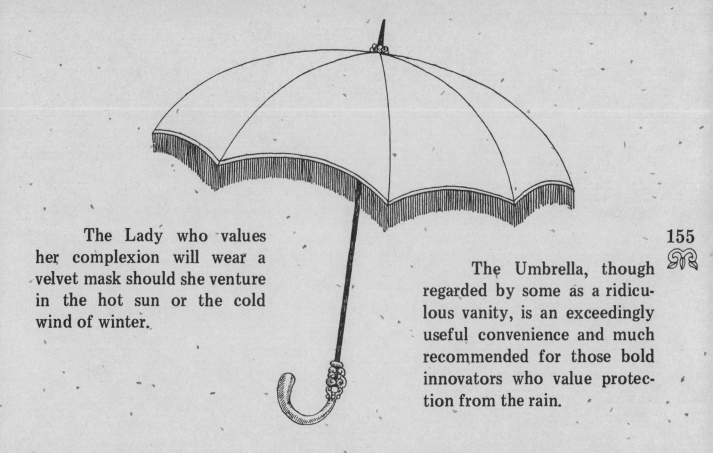

The Lady who values her complexion will wear a velvet mask should she venture in the hot sun or the cold wind of winter.

155

The Umbrella, though regarded by some as a ridiculous vanity, is an exceedingly useful convenience and much recommended for those bold innovators who value protection from the rain.

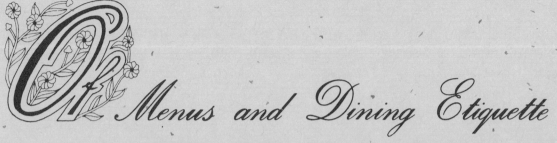

Of Menus and Dining Etiquette

Always remember, elegance can be achieved without extravagance. For those who have the nicest Taste, a crowd of rich Things are apter to satiate, than to please the Palate and a few good Ingredients make the best Dishes.

Dinner being the grand solid meal of the day, is a matter of considerable importance; and a well-served table is a striking index of human resource.

Even the most careful supervision and effort is not always rewarded with gracious compliments. You may also experience the frustrations Col. Landon Carter has written on:

I never knew the like of my family for finding fault. At the same time they will not mend things when they might if they could. Every(one) speak well of my table but they who constantly live at it. If the meat is very fine, it is not done says one, altho Perhaps nobody eat hartier of it . . . If the sallad is fine, the melted butter it is mixed up with is rank altho every mouthfull of sallad is devoured . . . and so the good folk go on disparaging and devouring.

Turtle Soup
Broiled Salmon Steaks or New England Poached Salmon with Egg Sauce
Green Peas   Small Boiled New Potatoes in Jackets
Indian Pudding or Apple Pandowdy
Coffee   Tea   Cyder

159

The salmon along the eastern seaboard begin to run in late June and are readily available for Independence Day. Along with the first new potatoes, and early peas, this is the traditional New England fourth of July dinner.

Juliana Smith of New England wrote this letter to me during the Revolution.

"All the baking of pies & cakes was done at our house & we had the big oven heated & filled twice each day for three days before it was all done. Of course we could have no Roast Beef. None of us have tasted Beef this three years back as it all must go to the Army, & too little they get, poor fellows."

Talking of the vegetables ... "One which I do not believe you have yet seen. Uncle Simeon had imported the Seede from England just before the War began & only this Year was there enough for Table use. It is called Sellery & you eat it without cooking.

We did not rise from the Table until it was quite dark, & then when the dishes had been cleared away we all got round the fire as close as we could, & cracked nuts, & sang songs & told stories. At least some told & others listened ... You know nobody can exceed the two Grandmothers at telling tales of all the things they have seen themselves, & repeating those of the early years in New England."

160

THANKSGIVING DINNER

Haunch of Venison   Roast Chine of Pork

Roast Turkey   Pigeon Pasties   Roast Goose

Onions in Cream   Cauliflower   Squash

Potatoes   Raw Cellery

Mincemeat Pie   Pumpkin Pie   Apple Pie

Indian Pudding   Plum Pudding

Cyder

161

The author has not had the honour of having Christmas Dinner at Mount Vernon, but reports of various guests suggest this might be the menu.

An Onion Soup Call'd the King's Soup

Oysters on Half Shell   Broiled Salt Roe Herring   Boiled Rockfish

Roast Beef and Yorkshire Pudding   Mutton Chops

Roast Suckling Pig   Roast Turky with Chestnut Stuffing

162

Round of Cold Boiled Beef with Horse-radish Sauce

Cold Virginia Baked Ham

Lima Beans   Baked Acorn Squash   Baked Cellery with Slivered Almonds

Hominy Pudding   Candied Sweet Potatoes

Cantaloupe Pickle   Spiced Peaches in Brandy   Spiced Cranberries

Mincemeat Pie   Apple Pie   Cherry Pie   Chess Tarts

Blancmange   Plums in Wine Jelly   Snowballs   Indian Pudding

Great Cake   Ice Cream   Plum Pudding

Fruits   Nuts   Raisins

Port   Madeira

IN MATTERS OF CARVING

How we all must regret to hear some Persons, even of Quality say, "pray, carve up that Hen," or "halve that Plover" not considering how indiscreetly they talk. These are the proper Terms:

cut up a turky
rear a goose
unbrace a Mallard or duck
unlace a coney
wing a partridge or quail
allay a pheasant
dismember a hern
thigh a woodcock
display a crane
lift a swan.

163

The Comte de Volney dipped his quill in vinegar when he wrote this critique of American eating. I offer this unfair and venomous essay only to show you French scorn for our ways. Why then, dear reader, do we so slavishly follow the French style?

I will venture to say that if a prize were proposed for the scheme of a regimen most calculated to injure the stomach, the teeth, and the health in general, no better could be invented than that of the Americans. In the morning at breakfast, they deluge their stomach with a quart of hot water, impregnated with tea, or so slightly with coffee that it is mere colored water; and they swallow, almost without chewing, hot bread, half baked, toast soaked in butter, cheese of the fattest kind, slices of salt or hung beef, ham, etc., all of which are nearly insoluble. At dinner they have boiled pastes under the name of puddings, and the fattest are deemed the most delicious; all their sauces, even for roast beef, are melted butter; their turnips and potatoes swim in hog's lard, butter or fat; under the name of pie or pumpkin, their pastry is nothing but a greasy paste, never sufficiently baked. To digest these viscous substances they take tea almost

164

instantly after dinner, making it so strong that it is absolutely bitter to the taste, in which state it affects the nerves so powerfully that even the English find it brings on a more obstinate restlessness than coffee. Supper again introduces salt meats or oysters. The whole day passes in heaping indigestions on one another; and to give tone to the poor, relaxed and wearied stomach, they drink Madeira, rum, French brandy, gin, or malt spirits, which complete the ruin of the nervous system.

TEA ETIQUETTE

I am amused at how many French visitors fail to understand one of the nuances of American etiquette, I mean our "tea signal." Of course the proper hostess continues to refill the tea-cup until it is turned upside down in the saucer and the spoon placed on top. I recently had occasion to take tea with company including a Frenchman who spoke no English and knew nothing of our sign language. He was so distressed to see the sixth cup arriving, after emptying it he put it into his pocket!

The founders of our Republic are accustomed to sitting down to magnificent feasts. It is not unusual for them to be offered soup, oysters, several varieties of fish, roasted turky, chicken, duck and goose, beef and mutton, beautiful molded jellies, puddings, pies, cakes, tarts, and all in one meal. Yet each of them have their own particular favorite meals and stiles of dining. The author has learned a few of them.

166 JOHN ADAMS

While he labored in Philadelphia he wrote his wife about the grand dinners he was invited to attend. To appease his conscience he called them "sinful feasts." At his own home, however, the frugal Mr. Adams is reported to have as his Sunday dinner: first course, pudding of Indian meal, molasses and butter, Second course, veal and bacon, mutton and vegetables. Besides these viands, the Adamses have beer and cider to drink.

BENJAMIN FRANKLIN

When he is at home in Philadelphia, Dr. Franklin's favorite breakfast is a bowl of porridge, sweetened with honey and spiced with nutmeg, accompanied by bread and butter and a cup of tea, and which he estimates costs three and one-halfpence.

While in London, Mrs. Franklin tells us his letters begged her to send him by the first packet out of Philadelphia the American foods for which he longed—apples, cranberries, dried peaches, buckwheat flour and corn meal.

THOMAS JEFFERSON

Few of his countrymen eat so well or are as interested in fine dining as is the author of the Declaration of Independence. He entertains grandly and has himself introduced some of the refinements of European cooking to America. From France he has brought receipts for blanc mange and meringues; from Holland he has born home a waffle iron; and from Italy he has brought a noodle called Neapolitan maccaroni. His knowledge and appreciation of the finest wines is renowned.

Unfairly, I believe, Mr. Thomas Paine has spoken of Mr. Jefferson's epicureanism as almost subversive. He claims Mr. Jefferson has "abjured his native victuals, neglecting good roast beef for delicacies of foreign inspiration."

I can assure the reader, for all his cosmopolitan tastes, he is still enthusiastic about his native foods: maple sugar, paccans, Virginia ham and beaten biscuits are some he has spoken of.

His favorite breakfast is most surely American: bacon and eggs, fried apples, and any of the Virginia hot breads which he loves.

GEORGE WASHINGTON

The General's favorite foods are mutton, shad, shrimp and oysters. For breakfast he likes salt herring, corncakes, honey and tea. While his guests have elaborate meals, he usually eats only one dish at dinner, accompanied by a cup of beer, but many glasses of wine.

John Adams in a letter to his Abigail in 1774 describes how delegates to the Continental Congress in Philadelphia enjoyed the local hospitality:

We go to congress at Nine, and there We stay, most earnestly engaged in Debates upon the most abstruse Misteries of State untill three in the Afternoon, then We adjourn, and go to Dinner with some of the Nobles of Pennsylvania, at four o Clock and feast upon ten thousand Delicacies, and sitt drinking Madeira, Claret and Burgundy till six or seven, and then go home, fatigued to death with Business, Company and Care ... I drink no Cyder, but feast upon Phyladelphia Beer, and Porter.

When General George Washington was but fifteen years he copied out these sensible and timeless rules. I recommend them to you.

Spit not in the Fire, nor Stoop low before it neither Put your Hands into the Flames to warm them, nor Set your Feet upon the Fire especially if there be meat before it . . . bedew no mans face with your Spittle, by approaching too near him when you Speak.

Kill no Vermin as Fleas, lice ticks &c in the Sight of Others, if you See any filth or thick Spittle put your foot Dexteriously upon it if it be upon the Cloths of your Companions, Put it off privately, and if it be upon your own Cloths return Thanks to him who puts it off.

171

Being Set at Meat scratch not neither Spit Cough or blow your Nose except there's a Necessity for it.

Cleanse not your teeth with the Table Cloth Napkin Fork or Knife but if Others do it let it be done with a Pick Tooth.

Promptness

Gen'l Washington had this remark for late arriving guests:

 *Gentlemen . . . I have a cook who never asks whether the company has come, but whether the hour has come.*

Elegant Behavior

A trifle was served at the close of a recent state dinner which, as everybody soon discovered, had been made with rancid cream. All the ladies began to watch Mrs. Washington to see what she would do—and, as was related all over town the next day, she was seen to taste and swallow her portion in self-martydrom.

Dignity Imperiled

A crisis in state-etiquette of the most painful sort has been much talked about recently. General Washington was touring New England and Governor Hancock, instead of calling upon the President, wrote Washington a most breezy note inviting him to stop at his house. When the invitation was declined he sent an even more breezy note asking the President to dine "en famille." The Gen'l again frostily refused and let it be known he would not see the Governor unless it was at his own lodgings. Such ultimatum having been given on Saturday evening with all the dignity of the Master of Mount Vernon, the Governor turned up bright and early Sunday with his respects. Reports are that seldom has Washington's traditional majesty been so nearly imperiled.

For the hostess who presumes to elegance, there are conventions and rules to be observed about the progression of dishes.

It is to be observed, that, in the Course of Dinners, the grosser Meats should always be set first on the Table; and there should never be two Dishes at a Dinner of the same Sort of Meat, tho; they are diversified by boiling one and roasting the other, or baking it; but make as much Variation as you can.

All boil'd Meats should be served first, baked Meats next, and roasted last.

... Boil'd Puddings of all Sorts, are for the first Course; but minc'd Pies, Tansies, Marrow Puddings, Orange Cakes, Lemon ditto, Almond ditto, and all other baked sweet Things, are for the second Course.

Pancakes ought always to come with the first Course, and Fritters.

Fashionable dinners of the day, especially in Virginia, are served at three o'clock in the afternoon, in three courses and on two tablecloths. One is removed between each course, and the fruits, nuts and wines are served on the bare table.

To please the eye as well as the palate, a balanced arrangement of dishes on the table is of first importance. It is a point of elegance that the table cloth should scarcely be visible. For varieties sake, the rule is nine dishes in each course for a dozen diners. For eighteen people, fifteen dishes.

Such is the fashion, but each hostess can follow as nearly as she wishes or is able.

The salt-cellar is the centerpiece of the table, especially in New England. Guests of honor are seated "above the salt," near the end of the table where the host and hostess sit side by side. Children and persons who are not of much account as guests are placed "below the salt."

When I was a child the fork was generally ridiculed as a little instrument "to make hay with our mouths," but it has now been adopted widely in the most genteel homes along with China instead of pewter.

TO HEAT A BED AT A MOMENTS NOTICE

Throw a little salt into the warming pan, and suffer it to burn for a minute previous to use.

A group of distinguished gentlemen recently gathered at the Coffee-House in New York to talk over navigation problems and also Mr. John Fitch's steamboat craft which has sailed the Delaware at twelve miles an hour! New York fashion writers recommend for such occasions that a pea-green coat with white vest and nankeen smallclothes would be proper, plus white silk stockings and pumps with silver buckles; the smallclothes to be tied at the knee with double bows.

176

The stories one hears of Southern hospitality are true I do believe. I have heard of a gentleman and his wife, who, being asked to dine at a residence on St. Simon, found that during the meal a boat had been sent to Darien, fifteen miles distant, for their luggage, and that so much pleased were host, hostess, and guests with one another, that their stay was prolonged until two children had been born to the visiting couple.

178

HOSPITALITY OF THE WASHINGTONS

Such a constant stream of guests visit Mount Vernon and are served elaborate meals in the Southern style, Washington has described it as a "well-resorted tavern." I have heard the food bills at the Presidential Table have mounted to $165.00 weekly! They are paid for by the Gen'l of course.

Though he is always hospitable, he wrote to a friend recently, "Unless someone pops in unexpectedly—Mrs. Washington and myself will do what I believe has not been done within the last twenty years by us—that is to set down to dinner by ourselves."

Finally, I commend to you this precept. Copy it out and tuck it where you will see it often.

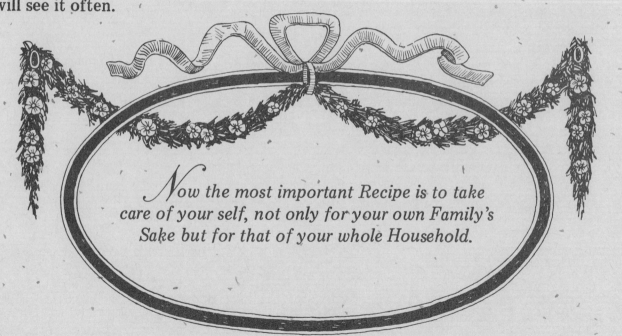

Now the most important Recipe is to take care of your self, not only for your own Family's Sake but for that of your whole Household.

Index

182

183